IMAGES
*of America*

# FORT DELAWARE

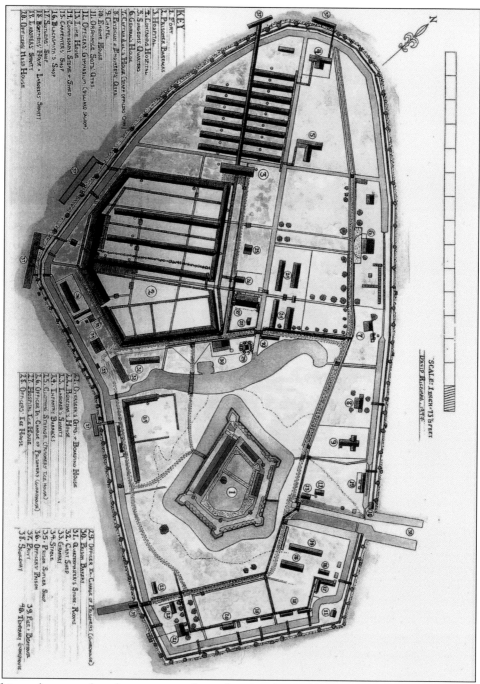

This modern map, based on engineer plans, photographs, and historical drawings, recreates the layout of Pea Patch Island in late 1864. (Plan by David W. Rickman.)

**ON THE COVER:** John Lawrence Gihon, a 25-year-old Philadelphia artist, photographed members of the Fort Delaware garrison in 1864. Seated from left to right are Morgan Jenkins, Joseph Boyd, Lt. Abraham G. Wolf, George Fleming, and Cpl. John Newland; (standing) William Calhoun, William Hardwick, Cpl. Emanuel M. Cockley, and Hampden McCreary. (Author's collection.)

IMAGES
*of America*

# FORT DELAWARE

Laura M. Lee and Brendan Mackie

ARCADIA
PUBLISHING

Published by Arcadia Publishing
Charleston, South Carolina

Printed in the United States of America

Library of Congress Control Number: 2009941878

For all general information contact Arcadia Publishing at:
Telephone 843-853-2070
Fax 843-853-0044
E-mail sales@arcadiapublishing.com
For customer service and orders:
Toll-Free 1-888-313-2665

Visit us on the Internet at www.arcadiapublishing.com

To Desmond Markey, *whose passion for history is contagious*

FINN'S POINT NATIONAL CEMETERY, FORT MOTT, N. J. In this beautiful cemetery are interred the remains of 2,628 Confederate and 135 Union soldiers, all but 113 of them being unknown. All the Confederates buried here died as prisoners of war at Fort Delaware, in the river opposite the cemetery. The monument shown on the left was erected in honor of the Union dead.

E. W. HUMPHREYS, PUBLISHER, WOODSTOWN, N. J.

This book is in honor of the over 2,650 prisoners of war, soldiers, and civilians that died on Pea Patch Island. Your sacrifice will not be forgotten. (Author's collection.)

# CONTENTS

As the war progressed, Fort Delaware's artillery batteries drilled in preparation for an attack that would never happen. Union victories in the war produced an increasing number of prisoners, rapidly filling already existing prison camps. Initially prisoner exchange between the North and South created a revolving door of sorts, but exchanges stalled. The South's refusal to treat captured black Union troops as soldiers, combined with the North's realization that they were fighting the same men over and over, created a backlog of prisoners for the Federal government.

The decision to transform the fort into a prison camp was not well received by its staff. Pea Patch was an ideal location not only because of its island status but also because it was an easily accessible site for prisoner exchanges. Surely the Union soldiers stationed at Fort Delaware were not particularly pleased about the addition of prison guard duties. The first prisoners to arrive at Fort Delaware, 250 men captured at the Battle of Kernstown, were housed within the fort's walls. Temporary barracks were hastily erected outside Fort Delaware not long after. By June of the same year, there was room for some 2,000 prisoners, with more barracks in the works for another 3,000. Brig. Gen. Albin Schoepf supervised construction of a prison compound on the western side of the island, thus creating accommodations for some 10,000 prisoners. The island's capacity was more than maxed out after Gettysburg and Vicksburg, when approximately 12,000 prisoners filled the barracks, while close to 13,000 total people resided on the island. In fact, a party held by Schoepf to celebrate completion of the barracks was interrupted by the arrival of 1,000 more rebels.

Fort Delaware was different from most other prison camps, housing enlisted men, officers, and political prisoners. Generally high-ranking officers and political prisoners resided in the interior of the fort, within the brick barracks rooms originally intended for the garrison. On rare occasions, Confederate officers attempted to hide their identity in an effort to stay with their men, but they were usually discovered. Lincoln's suspension of the writ of habeas corpus combined with patriotic fervor and general paranoia led to many ordinary citizens becoming "guests of the government." Sen. William Hitch of Laurel, Delaware, played Dixie on his trumpet in the town square, which landed him in Federal custody. A doctor making a comment while traveling by steamer ended up with a new destination—the prison camp. Reverend Handy, visiting relatives in nearby Port Penn, Delaware, made a comment about the flag that landed him at the fort for 15 months.

In three years, the island was home to over 32,000 prisoners. After the influx of Gettysburg and Vicksburg prisoners, the island population topped out at over 13,000 total people. Living conditions varied depending on the rank and prisoner status. High-ranking officers and some political prisoners are quoted in diaries and journals as having received ample supplemental provisions via packages and local sympathetic residents. The status of a regular enlisted man with no contacts in the north, however, was in stark contrast to the delicious dinners Reverend Handy discusses in his journal. Overall living conditions for both prisoners and garrison were obviously not optimal but must be examined in the context of 19th-century wartime. Prisoners often arrived in already weakened condition, suffering from diseases such as typhoid fever, scurvy, malaria, chronic diarrhea, and smallpox. Of the nearly 32,000 prisoners, over 2,400 Confederates never went home. Of that, nearly half of the deaths were in the second half of 1863, as a smallpox epidemic wracked the island. By November of that year, every man on the island had received a smallpox vaccine, sharply curbing the mortality. The majority of all deaths on the island were in fact due to disease; however, the death rate at Fort Delaware was actually lower than that on the battlefield. Surely Fort Delaware was no country club, but it provided a roof over their heads, medical care, and regular meals. Extensive quartermaster records document large purchases of food, and the hospital was one of the largest and most modern military facilities of its time. Likewise, it can be argued from the Union side that other prisons, such as Andersonville, had horribly inhumane conditions. Prisoners at Fort Delaware lived in barracks, while captives at Andersonville were essentially left to the elements. This occurred, however, in an atmosphere of war where the Confederacy was unable to provide adequate basics to their own civilians and army. The devastated economy and lack of provisions and supplies made war hell for everyone in the South.

The story of Fort Delaware is not complete if it only tells of those imprisoned or stationed there. The presence of the prison camp turned the sleepy island into the second largest city in Delaware. A prisoner of war post required guards, blacksmiths, carpenters, boatsmen, laundresses, artillerymen, doctors, infantrymen, ordinary laborers, and even a teacher. Workers brought their families, babies were born, surgeons lived on the island, and yes, people died there. Dr. Washington G. Nugent, post surgeon, described the staff quarters on officer's row as "a nice house . . . small but has a tasty neat cottage, they have an elegant garden adjoining the General's, and both they and General Schoepf have any quantity of fine grapes, also a fine flower garden." Images of the east side of the island show the house replete with a grape arbor, a screened porch, and white picket fence. Meanwhile, on the west side, prisoners were doing their laundry, bathing, and washing dishes in the muck of stagnant drainage ditches.

Four months after the conclusion of the war, the prison camp ceased operation with the exception of high-profile Confederates and some Federal convicts. Burton N. Harrison, Jefferson Davis's personal secretary, was the last Confederate to be released. Fort Delaware as a fortification was now obsolete due to advances in weaponry. By 1870, the garrison was removed from the island, and the post was in the hands of the U.S. Army Corps of Engineers. Fort Delaware suffered the ravages of time over the next 35 years; storms and time were its enemies. Repairs were made to the damage, but funds were insufficient. Modernization efforts to the post included modifying the barbette platforms and construction of service magazines on the parapet.

Between 1870 and 1899, Fort Delaware was yet again modernized as part of a national effort to improve coastal defenses. Fifteen-inch Rodman guns were added less than 10 years after the Civil War, and a torpedo casemate to control river mines was added in 1892. The improvements were in coordination with Forts Mott and DuPont, rounding out the three-point system of defense. A reinforced concrete battery on the south end, named Battery Torbert, was constructed from 1898 to 1899. It contained three 12-inch guns hidden from river view by disappearing carriages, with a range of 8 miles. Rapid-fire guns were added as well. By 1901, Fort Delaware was once again garrisoned, but only in a secondary role as an outpost of Fort DuPont. By 1904, the Fort Delaware garrison was removed, and the island returned to the U.S. Army Corps of Engineers. The river was dredged, and nearly 1 million cubic feet of dredge spoils were dumped on the island, raising its level approximately 5 to 10 feet. After allowing the spoils to settle for about four years, a small detachment was sent to the island as a garrison during World War I. From the end of World War I to the beginning of World War II, the fort's role, according to Edward W. Cooch in *Delaware, A Guide to the First State*, was to "warn off trespassers, to paint mines and other equipment, and to care for the modern guns." By June 1942, World War II necessitated another enlargement of the garrison. However, the completion of Fort Miles in Lewes, Delaware, rendered Fort Delaware to permanent mothball status. In 1943, the 12-inch guns went to Watervleit Arsenal, and Fort Delaware's Civil War pieces were scrapped.

From Fort Delaware's declaration as surplus in 1945 until it was turned over to the Delaware State Park Commission in 1951, the site was systematically picked apart by scavengers and souvenir hunters. A group of concerned citizens with an endearing love of history and the old fort formed the Fort Delaware Society in an effort to spur preservation. Their tireless effort resulted in preservation of numerous historical records pertaining to Fort Delaware. Since that time, the Fort Delaware Society and Delaware State Parks have worked in coordination to preserve the site and educate the public about its unique role in Delaware history. Were it not for the dedication of a few ruthless amateur historians back in 1951, it is likely that Fort Delaware's fate would be quite different from the state park it is today.

Marc Bloch studied medieval history and was a French army captain in World War II. Killed by the Gestapo following his efforts for the French Resistance, he once said that "history is neither watchmaking nor cabinet construction. It is an endeavor toward better understanding." Fort Delaware historical records include a treasure trove of photographs, maps, sketches, diaries, journals, memoirs, newspaper articles, and family histories. Unfortunately, it is not an exact science or craft. These tools enable the student of history to travel back in time and attempt to arrive at an understanding of what it was like to live, work, or be a captive at Fort Delaware. A fort resident writing his memoir 30 years after the war may not have as accurate a recollection as someone who wrote home to his wife in 1862. However, history is about taking all of these puzzle pieces and trying to arrive at that comprehensive understanding. It is about historians sharing their information for their better good, to help all understand what Fort Delaware was about. A description of the barracks by a prisoner can be compared to a photograph of the structure or blueprints taken from the official records documenting its construction.

Susan Sontag once said that "Life is not significant details, illuminated by a flash, fixed forever. Photographs are." Within this book are some of the photographs, sketches, blueprints, and letters that piece together the story of Fort Delaware. They support and help bring meaning to the documentary sources that breathe life into this significant period of Delaware history.

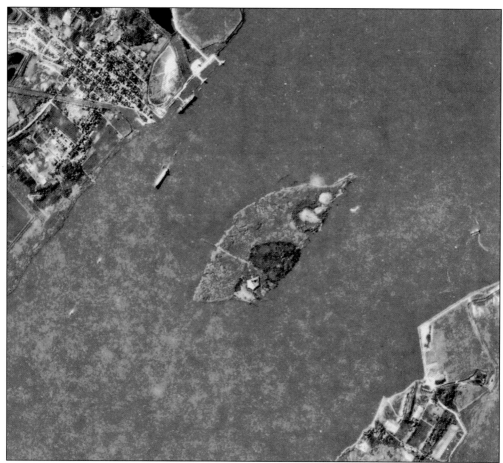

A satellite image shows Fort Delaware on Pea Patch Island, Fort Mott in New Jersey (lower right), and Fort DuPont (left) and Delaware City (upper left) on the Delaware side. One hundred fifty years before this image was taken, Maj. Benjamin Kendrick Pierce wrote home about the February 8-9, 1831, fire that destroyed the star fort. "The crashing of the falling timbers, the bright flames streaming to the skies and the interspersed thundering explosions of the powder that had been thrown outside presented a scene awfully sublime, but for me it presented neither attraction, nor terror—neither splendour, magnificence nor awe, I saw . . . that we had a herculean task before us and conducted myself accordingly, encouraging and rousing the men to continue, and as the danger pressed, to increase exertion. (Delaware State Parks.)

# One

# DEFENDING THE DELAWARE
## 1813–1860

In 1784, a survey of Pea Patch was conducted by the deputy surveyor of New Jersey, Elnathan Davis. Edward and Clement Hall claimed ownership, dating back to 1743 and 1782 property warrants. They rented the island to John Mugway for two years for 50 muskrat skins a year or $12.50. In 1813, they sold the island to Dr. Henry Gale for $500, but others laid claim to Pea Patch as well.

The War of 1812 and British river threats sent citizens into a panic. The government offered Dr. Gale $30,000 for the island, which he refused. In response, the commander of the U.S. Military District No. 5 approached the State of Delaware instead. After legal wrangling, it was determined it was indeed state property. Soon after, the state ceded its title to the United States.

Laborers were sent to "erect a work, of earth (or more durable materials, if found advisable). . . . The plan and extent of the work will be adapted to the relation which the island bears to the shores and channel of the Delaware." Capt. Thomas Clark of the engineers constructed an embankment wall that reclaimed submerged portions of the island. Efforts to fortify the island with earthworks were followed by construction on the star-shaped fort. However, by 1822, the project went awry, as the structure's weight taxed the marshy land. Amidst efforts to reinforce the foundation and patch cracking walls, a devastating fire of 1831 abruptly ended the future of the fort.

Another dispute over island ownership stalled efforts to construct a second fort. Joseph Hudson now claimed ownership of the island, tying up progress for over 10 years. The courts found in favor of Hudson, who sold the island to the government for $1,005.

Thus another effort began to construct fortifications on Pea Patch—the structure that survives today. This effort included over 12,000 piles driven into the ground, some driven one over the other. Pilings extended nearly 60 feet into the mud and were stress tested to ensure adequate strength. Grillage timbers were laid in tiers over the piles. Shops and quarters were built, stair towers and cisterns were installed, and iron rails were laid for gun rooms. By 1858, the new Fort Delaware was ready for artillery and its future as a military post.

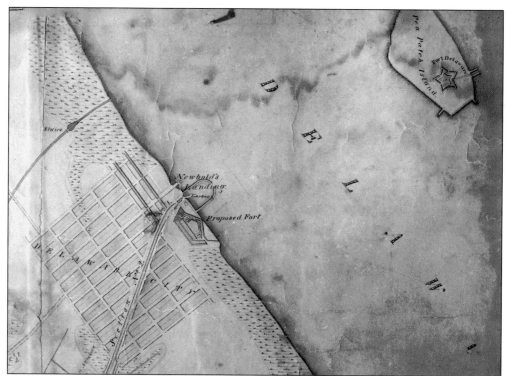

Fort Delaware, Pea Patch Island, and Delaware City appear on a Chesapeake and Delaware Canal map around 1829. Pea Patch Island was chosen early as an ideal location for harbor defense on the Delaware River. Delaware City was essential to the subsistence of an island fortification, providing military and civilian inhabitants with necessary resources. (Delaware State Parks.)

The small port town of Delaware City, founded in the 1820s, is located at the mouth of the eastern branch of the Chesapeake and Delaware Canal. Ships used the town's lock (above) to navigate between the river and the branch canal. Everything from agriculture to lumber, fuel, cattle, and mail was transported in passing vessels. (Fort Delaware Society.)

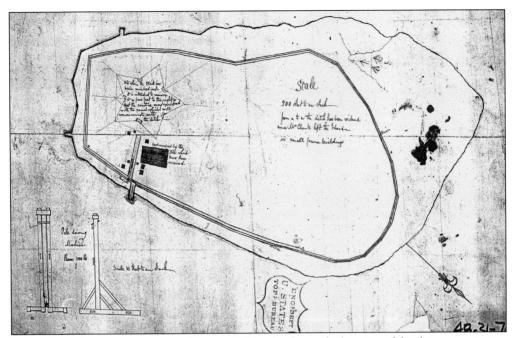

Babcock's early engineering plans of Pea Patch Island indicate the location of the sluice gate, staging area for the wooden piles, and initial planned placement of the star fort. Babcock's written notes indicate the fort's tentative location, which would subsequently be shifted to properly align with the sluice. Construction involved stabilizing the island's marsh environment using the wooden piles and engineering a system of drainage ditches to solidify the island. (National Archives.)

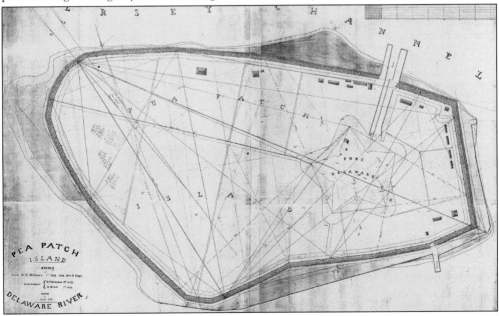

The fort's pentagonal construction consisted of casemated masonry walls, brownstone, and lumbered interior buildings. "Because of inadequate pilings and grillage, uneven settling of the masonry provided ongoing construction problems and delayed the completion . . . years past the proposed date." (Plans by Lt. W. G. Williams, courtesy of National Archives.)

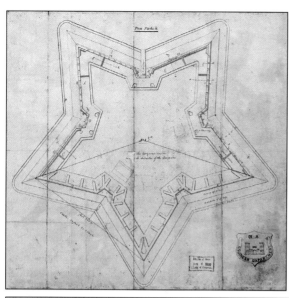

The unstable nature of the marsh environment and below-sea-level ground surface wreaked havoc on the foundation of the fort and the garrison's health. In 1825, Maj. Andrew Fanning, commander of the fort, wrote to the secretary of war advising him as to the health concerns. Fanning was permitted to vacation his 2nd U.S. Artillery soldiers at Cape May, New Jersey, until the hot season was over. Maj. Benjamin K. Pierce and an initial company of the 4th U.S. Artillery would later replace Major Fanning and his troops. (National Archives.)

*The burning of Fort Delaware.*—This event which we announced on Saturday morning, in a letter from a correspondent, says the N. Y. Journal of Commerce of the 14th inst. is stated in the Philadelphia Chronicle to have been caused by a stove pipe, passing through the roof of Lt. Tuttle's quarters. It is added, that the quarters of the soldiers and officers, except those of the commander and engineers, with much clothing, provision, and furniture, have been destroyed ; and that the work now is but the mere skeleton of a fortification. The public loss is estimated at ONE HUNDRED THOUSAND DOLLARS.

Fort Delaware is situated on Pea Patch Island, an island of recent formation in the river Delaware, and has been usually garrisoned with two companies of artillery.

On February 8, 1831, around 10:30 p.m., the fort suffered a devastating fire, originating in Lt. Stephen Tuttle's quarters. The blaze consumed Tuttle's room, rapidly spreading to the rest of the fort's adjoining interior woodwork. The powder magazines' high explosives were hastily removed, while others attempted a vain effort to save the structure. News spread nationwide documenting the total destruction of the fort. On the morning of February 9, the soldiers and civilians of Fort Delaware were forced to evacuate and sought refuge in Delaware City. (Fort Delaware Society.)

Maj. Benjamin Pierce had two losses to deal with. In addition to the fort's destruction, his wife Amanda Boykin Pierce, ill since December, passed away on January 17, 1831. Due to inclement weather, her body was still on the island during the blaze. Pierce wrote, "the remains of my dear Amanda was deposited in one of the magazines, the doors and wooden work of which caught fire, and expecting that the coffin and body would be burnt, I took four men and rushed through a solid sheet of fire and brought it out on the center of the parade [grounds] where it was preserved." (Photograph by Brendan Mackie.)

After the fire, Amanda Pierce was buried at the Immanuel Episcopal Church, located upriver in nearby New Castle, Delaware. Founded in 1689, Immanuel Episcopal Church is one of the oldest parishes in the country. Amanda is buried along with two Pierce children: Henry Jackson (died March 3, 1830) and Benjamin Kendrick Jr. (died August 26, 1831). (Delaware Public Archives.)

Pierce wrote that "There is at New Castle an Arsenal belonging to the United States, unoccupied and a fine building . . . to accommodate two Companies of Men and in the Village. . . . Quarters for the Officers may be rented cheap. This perhaps may be considered the most eligible situation for this command until Fort Delaware can be reoccupied." His suggestion was granted, and the arsenal served as barracks until 1832. Note the Immanuel Church steeple, seen behind the arsenal's roof. (Photograph by Brendan Mackie.)

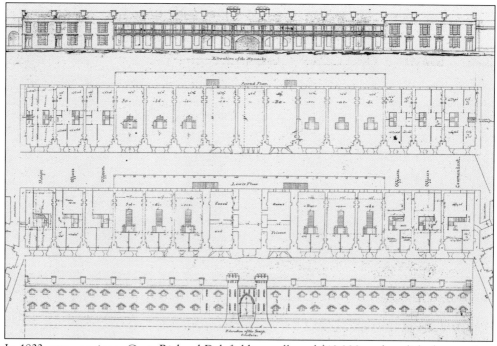

In 1833, army engineer Capt. Richard Delafield was allotted $10,000 to demolish the star fort. New fort construction followed but was interrupted by another legal battle over island ownership. A 10-year dispute over possession ensued, with the Circuit Court of the United States making the final decision. The government paid the plaintiff for the island, and construction resumed in 1848. (Plans by Richard Delafield, courtesy of National Archives.)

In 1846, Brevet Maj. John Sanders, army engineer and West Point graduate, arrived on Pea Patch Island to supervise construction of the new Fort Delaware. "Remnants of the Delafield fort were in ruins after the ten-year hiatus in construction." Major Sanders and his men "required almost eighteen months to clear the rotted wooden debris away and excavate the drainage ditches." Captain Delafield's 1830s fortification plans were scrapped. Major Sanders's superior, Chief Engineer Joseph Totten, devised an improved foundation plan, complimented by an equally reliable design for the actual fort. (Fort Delaware Society.)

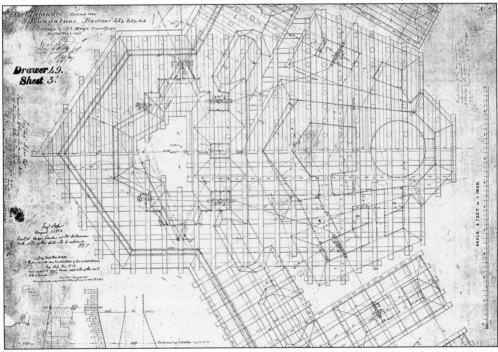

Engineer plans detail the strategic layout of both the wooden piles and grillage platform. Totten and Sanders tested the weight resistance of each pile by a series of blows. Construction on the fort would not progress until the foundation was proven sound. A total of 6,006 piles were utilized in the initial construction. (Sketch by Lt. Montgomery Meigs, courtesy of National Archives.)

Above, a refurbished Delafield steam-powered pile driver works on Fort Delaware's foundation. With the island flooded and the drivers modified, the massive lumbered piles were easier to position and drive into place. (Fort Delaware Society.)

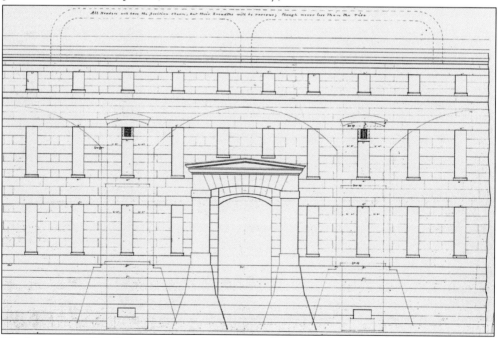

The front view of Fort Delaware shows the use of granite columns and arches designed to properly distribute the weight and thus minimize any foundation issues. (National Archives.)

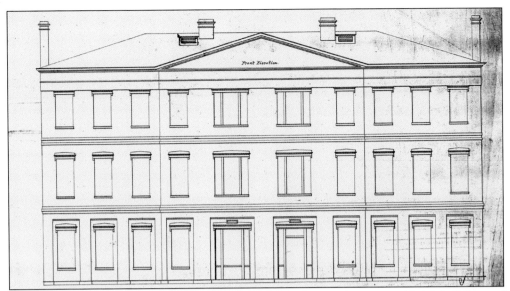

Interior construction plans (above) included the layout for two three-storied brick buildings, of identical design, which served as officer quarters. The ground floors had kitchens, with residences on the second and third level. Another, longer building, similar in appearance, was planned for soldier barracks. (National Archives.)

In 1851, army engineer Capt. George B. McClellan reported to Major Sanders for duty on Pea Patch Island. McClellan appears in the daguerreotype above, standing on the extreme right. Seated next to McClellan is Richard Delafield, the island's earlier engineer. (Library of Congress.)

Brevet Brig. Gen. Joseph G. Totten was appointed Chief Engineer of the U.S. Army in 1838. During fort construction, Brigadier General Totten constantly communicated with Major Sanders regarding all engineering issues. It was estimated that Fort Delaware would be ready for armament and garrison between 1858 and 1859. (Library of Congress.)

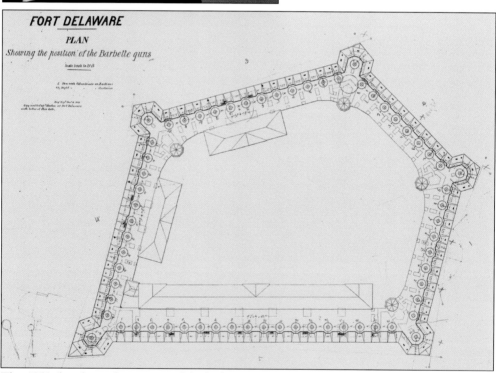

This 1858 plan shows the position of the barbette guns on the third tier and also shows the outline of interior barracks and twin officer quarters. Major Sanders did not live to see the heavy guns mounted; he passed away on Pea Patch Island around July 29, 1858. (National Archives.)

# Two

# From Protector to Prison

## The Civil War Years

By 1861, forty-seven guns were mounted, and a small garrison of the 4th U.S. Artillery manned the fort under Capt. Augustus Gibson. Garrison drilled in preparation for oncoming conflict the same year and into 1862. Fort Delaware watched for the Confederate ironclad *Virginia*, rumored to be a possible threat to Delaware River shipping. But by April, the government was thinking more about the fort's potential as a prisoner-of-war camp than as a defensive fortification.

Prison barracks for 10,000 were constructed outside of the fort walls by mid-1863. They filled rapidly after Federal victories at Gettysburg and Vicksburg. Said Capt. J. W. Hibbs, "Our barracks a miniature world is not so much of a misnomer as it might seem to be at first to the uninitiated." The compound had kitchens, a bakery, sutler shop, and a nearby hospital. The bullpen, or open area of the barracks, was the source of much daily activity. Prisoners played chess, made jewelry out of buttons and peach pits, and earned extra money cutting hair or doing laundry for fellow prisoners. Some worked as ditch diggers, as carpenters, or hauling wood. There was a theatrical society, Christian Commission, poetry club, and even a prison newspaper, *Prison Times*.

The "sinks" or privies were outside the compound, emptying directly into the river. This was a popular escape route, but departures were curbed by the presence of rooftop lanterns as well as strategically located guards. Official records indicate some 300 prisoners escaped throughout the course of the war. Navigating the river current was a challenge; though many attempted it, few succeeded. Men used canteens as makeshift life preservers, usually to no avail. By 1864, the prison population was essentially maxed out, and the numbers held relatively steady until the end of the war.

The pictorial record from this period of Fort Delaware's existence is a wonderful source of information thanks in part to the popularity of the photographic image. Union soldiers, civilians, and even Confederate prisoners had their likenesses taken, and many are preserved in the historical record. Photographer John Lawrence Gihon's visits to the island were mentioned in diaries and memoirs of both prisoners and guards. One might wonder why a Confederate officer held captive at the fort would be posing with a sword in his hand, but it probably speaks volumes as to the respect and trust they received from their captors.

Topographical engineer H. von Steinaecker included the ongoing construction of the counterscarp, mounted barbette guns, and the newly raised roof of the soldier barracks in his watercolor of Fort Delaware. By February 1861, twenty regular army soldiers under the command of Capt. Augustus A. Gibson garrisoned the fort. (Delaware Historical Society.)

Collis' Zouaves de Afrique was one of the first volunteer units to arrive on Pea Patch Island after the war started. The Zouaves were quite a spectacle with their flashy attire resembling that of French troops serving in North Africa during the 1830s. The independent infantry company remained at Fort Delaware only a short time before heading to the front. (West Point Museum.)

Capts. Stanislaus Mlotkowski (left) and Paul T. Jones (seated) pose with two unidentified individuals. In 1861, Stanislaus Mlotkowski arrived as a lieutenant in Battery A, Independent Pennsylvania Heavy Artillery. Mlotkowski was promptly promoted to captain following the resignation of his superior, Frank Schaffer. During the war, his battery served at the fort longest, remaining until June 1865. Jones's battery arrived in early 1862, remaining only a few months. After transfer, his battery became Company L, 2nd Pennsylvania Heavy Artillery. (Delaware State Parks.)

Capt. J. S. Jarden 2ᵈ Penna. Artillery - (112ᵗʰ Regt.) died suddenly on the 8ᵗʰ Novr. 1863 at Fort Thayer near Washington DC. Loved by his men, a favorite with his brother officers, and a model officer we mourn his loss.

Yours Capt. Jno. S. Jarden

Batteries D, G, and H, 2nd Pennsylvania Heavy Artillery garrisoned Fort Delaware from January to March 1862. Lt. John S. Jarden of Battery H later accepted promotion to captain of Battery C. He would not survive the war. (Author's collection.)

Capt. Augustus A. Gibson, a West Point graduate and Mexican War veteran, foresaw the critical need for additional artillery and garrison in the face of war. He commanded a fort with only 47 guns mounted, lacking adequate garrison, and the new headache of accommodating Confederate prisoners. On July 16, 1862, Gibson reported "Nineteen prisoners escaped last night. . . . It is impossible to prevent escapes without a larger force. I ask for re-enforcements immediately." (Delaware State Parks.)

Prisoners were frequently the recipient of supplies and comforting letters sent by sympathetic women from the North. Lt. Benjamin G. Patterson, 7th Virginia Cavalry, conveyed his thanks to Julia A. Jefferson of New Castle, Delaware. Patterson was a prisoner at Fort Delaware not once but twice. (Photograph by John L. Gihon, courtesy of Fort Delaware Society.)

By the summer of 1862, prisoners were permitted to write letters but could only correspond within states still in the Union. Prison mail was censored by Federal soldiers on the island, then went through the suddenly overworked Delaware City post office. (Delaware State Parks.)

Gilbert S. Clark, a lieutenant in Franz von Schilling's Battery B, Marine and Fortification Artillery (a fancy name for Heavy Artillery) models the naval-like uniform of his unit. The "marine artillery" served at Fort Delaware from February 1862 to May 1863. Clark was detached, promoted to captain, and remained at the fort as quartermaster and later post commissary officer. He mustered out as a major in 1865. (Delaware State Parks.)

Lt. John Krause, Battery A, Marine Artillery (John S. Stevenson's battery) started the war guarding prisoners and later found himself as one. In 1864, while engaged in North Carolina, Confederate forces captured Krause and a detachment of his men. After two months as a POW, Krause was exchanged and returned to his unit. Krause survived the war, but the majority of his men died at the infamous Andersonville prison camp. (Photograph by Samuel Broadbent, author's collection.)

Pvt. Duane L. Tyler of Capt. David Schooley's Independent Battery started his army career at Fort Delaware in August 1862. Private Tyler and his unit remained at the fort until November 1862 before heading to Fort Lincoln. Schooley's Battery became Company M of the 2nd Pennsylvania Heavy Artillery. Capt. Augustus Gibson accepted a commission as colonel of the 2nd Pennsylvania, also ending his tenure at the fort. (Photograph by B. P. Paige, courtesy of Ron Coddington.)

**Pea Patch Island,** independently of the Fort, is not a spot of intense interest. Its staple products are willows and marsh grass, varied by occasional lawns, small gardens and white cottages. Among these dwellings may be mentioned that of General NEWTON, the boarding house of Mrs. OGLE, for officers, and that of Mrs. GUNNING, for laborers. In addition is that of Mr. MUHLENBROOK, in charge of the engineering department, and those of Mr. JOHN B. WELCH, the Sutler, of several army employees, and of four washerwomen. A small burying ground in one corner contains twelve graves of Rebel prisoners. Union soldiers who die on the island are taken home. The spot is healthy; the sanitary regulations strict, and deaths are rare.

Descriptions of the island were many, from newspaper articles to letters home. Julia Schoepf, wife of Gen. Albin Schoepf, described her "island home" as "large and airy, a perfect gem, with many closets, a garden adorned with graceful vines, beautiful and delicious fruit trees in profusion and river scenery." She also added that "the beautiful with the terrible beclouds our background," obviously referring to the prison camp. (Fort Delaware Society.)

The steamer *Major Reybold*, built in 1852, was named after prominent Delaware City resident Maj. Philip Reybold. An entrepreneur and successful peach farmer, Reybold was well known as the "Peach King." The *Major Reybold*, a fixture of Delaware City, transported civilians, soldiers, and Confederate prisoners bound for Pea Patch Island. The ship ran regular routes between Philadelphia and Salem. The 461-ton, iron-hulled steamer, built by Harlan and Hollingsworth, was in service until 1908. (Author's collection.)

On August 23, 1862, Pvt. Harry Gosser (left) and the rest of Captain Young's Independent Battery G, Pittsburgh Heavy Artillery arrived at Fort Delaware. Pvt. Alexander J. Hamilton (also Battery G), wrote that they "marched down Arch Street and put aboard the Steamer Major Reybold . . . had a very pleasant trip down the Delaware River . . . Arrived at Fort Delaware about six, were kept waiting outside for some time then marched into the fort and were given quarters in an unfinished room." (Photograph by Harbaugh and Green, author's collection.)

In the fall of 1862, Maj. Henry S. Burton, Gibson's replacement, stands with his battery commanders (all captains) inside Fort Delaware. From left to right are John Jay Young, Franz Wilhelm von Schilling, Paul T. Jones, Maj. Henry S. Burton, John S. Stevenson, Stanislaus Mlotkowski, and David Schooley. This is the earliest known existing Fort Delaware photograph. (Delaware Historical Society.)

On May 16, 1863, Cpl. Bishop Crumrine (Battery G) wrote, "I will [send] you a picture of the finest Fort in the U.S. to-morrow. It was taken when there were but few guns mounted on the parapet yet it is a good picture. The Fort is being sodded on the inside and it looks like a flower garden. Our rooms are all plastered and fixed up nicely." (Photograph by T.G. Holland, courtesy of Fort Delaware Society.)

Officers gather around June 7, 1863, outside the fort at the staff officer quarters. From left to right are Lt. William Hall, Capt. Stanislaus Mlotkowski, Lt. John MacConnell, Capt. William Kesley, Maj. Henry Burton, Capt. John Young, Capt. Aaron Carter, Lt. Thomas Ashton, unidentified, Lt. Alfred Herr, Lt. George Ahl, Lt. August Reinecke, and Lt. Charles Hawkins. Lieutenant Hall wears the hat, sword, and epaulets presented to him on May 26, 1863, following promotion. Captain Carter and Lieutenant Ashton are from Company C, 157th Pennsylvania Infantry, which left by July 1863. Private Hamilton notes on June 7, "among a pleasure party is a photographer taking views of the island. Company C and Battery G went out and were photographed." The following day he notes "an expedition under the command of Major Burton left on the *Liberty* in search of blockade runner." (Delaware Historical Society.)

On June 20, 1863, Private Hamilton wrote in his diary that "five hundred of the Fifth Delaware [Infantry] came here for duty." Capt. Lammot duPont, of Company B, was notorious for patenting "B" blasting powder in 1857. The 5th Delaware guarded prisoners until departing the island on August 6, 1863. Lammot duPont survived the war but was killed in a gunpowder explosion on March 29, 1884. (Delaware Historical Society.)

THE ARRIVAL OF TWO THOUSAND VICKSBURG PRISONERS AT FORT DELAWARE.—[Sketched by Mr. D. Auld, Forty-thi……

Pvt. David Auld, 43rd Ohio Infantry, documents the *Liberty* disembarking rebels and Fort Delaware's east side. On June 9, 1863, Private Hamilton noted "a large lot of prisoners arrived from Vicksburg." The next day "the band had a ball at the new barracks, a large crowd of ladies are present, and they are having a gay time. Thanks to wine and liquor, many of the boys are jolly, and most of the officers are drunk. Among us a party of Ohioans who came in guard of the prisoners. I met an old acquaintance, Henry Bruner" of the 43rd Ohio Infantry. (Delaware Public Archives.)

In 1863, William Cannon was elected governor of Delaware after defeating Democratic candidate Samuel Jefferson in a very contentious election that included armed troops at the polling places. In August 1863, Hamilton's diary mentioned that the governor was "sightseeing around [the island], and the General [Schoepf] escorted him to Wilmington in the evening." Governor Cannon died in office in March 1865. (Delaware Historical Society.)

Brig. Gen. Albin Francisco Schoepf commanded Fort Delaware from April 1863 until January 1866. Schoepf, a combat veteran, was well respected by his Confederate prisoners. Basil Duke described him as "a fine, stalwart, kindly old Hungarian." Isaac Handy thought Schoepf "a tall man, and rather good looking." Elwood Garrett, son of abolitionist Thomas Garrett, photographed Schoepf in 1863. Schoepf presented his likeness to Capt. Lammot duPont while stationed at Fort Delaware. (Fort Delaware Society.)

> Fort Delaware, Del.
> July 17 1863.
>
> Miss Jefferson.
>         I have the honor to acknowledge the receipt of quite a large amount of delicacies, eatables, and pillows for the use of hospital. Accept the thanks of the Genl commanding, Dr Silliman and myself, for your kindness.
>         Genl Trimble is not here. You can send Genl Archer the articles you wrote about.
>         The officers will all leave here to morrow morning. Dr Silliman wishes to return his thanks for the kind offer of the ladies to come down and assist him, and says, that it will not be necessary for them to come, as he has plenty of assistance.
>                     My Respectfully,
>                     D. G. MacConnell
>                     2 Lt Adjt

Following the Gettysburg campaign, the majority of captured Confederates were sent to Fort Delaware. Brig. Gen. James J. Archer, a Maryland native, was one of over 8,000 rebels to arrive in July 1863. The above letter illustrates the interest sparked by Archer's arrival. (Fort Delaware Society.)

Maj. Gen. Franklin Gardner, a New York native, was another high-ranking Confederate who resided for a time at Fort Delaware. Gardner, a West Point graduate, surrendered following the fall of Port Hudson. Gardner was exchanged in August 1864. During the war, a dozen high-ranking Confederate generals were held at Fort Delaware, including Johnston Pettigrew, Edward Johnson, George Steuart, Jeff Thompson, Rufus Barringer, John Jones, Thomas Churchill, Robert Page, and Joseph Wheeler. (Library of Congress.)

Rev. Isaac W. K. Handy of Portsmouth, Virginia, was a political prisoner held at the fort for 15 months. A Presbyterian minister who once served the congregation of Port Penn, he was visiting his wife's family in Delaware when he made a comment about the flag over dinner. The comment landed in a local newspaper, and Reverend Handy soon landed in Fort Delaware. Handy refused to take the Oath of Allegiance despite several opportunities. He found his calling at the fort, ministering to the prisoners on a daily basis. (Photograph by John L. Gihon, courtesy of Fort Delaware Society.)

In July 1863, Pvt. Alexander Hamilton wrote, "The fort is a strong work of bricks and granite. It has five equal or nearly equal sides, the angles being rendered acute by strong bastions. It contains three stories or tiers of guns. . . . The work has the capacity of mounting sixty-four barbette, sixty-six casemate, and twenty-two bastion guns, in all, one hundred and fifty-two." (Lithograph by Thomas Sinclair, courtesy of Fort Delaware Society.)

Rebecca Dilworth Handy, wife of Rev. Isaac Handy, was afforded visitation rights several times during the war. Reverend Handy noted "The safety of the manuscript is due to the preserving care of my wife, who received it in numbers, by such 'underground' opportunities as were constantly afforded." This image was found in the personal album of Lydia A. Jefferson, daughter of Democratic candidate Samuel Jefferson. (Photograph by Frederick F. Gutekunst, courtesy of Fort Delaware Society.)

The Jefferson House, located on the Strand in New Castle, Delaware, was the original store and residence of Elihu Jefferson and his daughter Julia A. Jefferson. Julia, along with her cousin Lydia A. Jefferson, were just two of many women from the area who provided aid to the prisoners. Citizens who provided necessities for the prisoners were often characterized as "Copperheads" (Southern sympathizers). Most of the aid groups cited altruistic motives in response to prison overcrowding. The women corresponded with many of the men, not only during the war but after as well. (Photograph by Brendan Mackie.)

"The new barracks, immediately in front of the fort and just opposite our window, are now nearly completed. The building, which is between 500 and 600 feet long, has been put up entirely by our Southern soldiers, who have been promised 40 cents a day for their labor," according to Rev. Isaac Handy on August 27, 1863. (Delaware State Parks.)

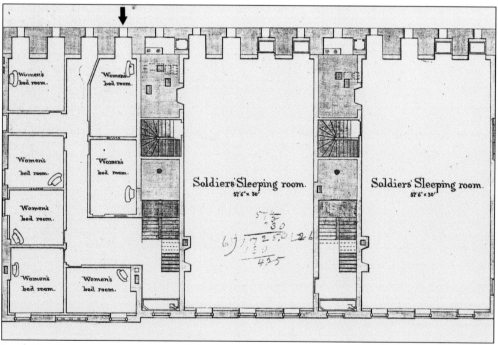

Inside Fort Delaware, the main barracks had separate apartments originally intended for laundresses. Many rooms inside the fort were converted to house political prisoners and Confederate officers. Handy wrote, "I decided to quarter in No. 6 . . . I made myself acquainted in nearly all the rooms, which I find to be seven in number, each of them opening upon one of the two passages in this apartment." He went on to say, "this room is, perhaps, 12 by 18 feet, with an alcove, and grated window; the latter opening to the southwest, and looking directly across the water to Delaware City." (National Archives.)

"We have to wash our hands, faces, and feet in the sluggish ditch-water which runs through the campus, and a good many strip to their waists and bathe themselves. . . . Beer, made of fermented corn meal and cheap or mean molasses, and weak lemonade are sold at various stands made of boxes . . . there is a tent of sutler's supplies near the mess hall, kept by an avaricious Yankee. Tobacco, matches, oil for cooking lamps, stationery, bakers bread, pies, cakes, apples, onions, etc. all of very poor quality, are kept for sale," according to Capt. Robert E. Park, 12th Alabama Infantry. (Delaware State Parks.)

Sgt. Charles James French, 9th Virginia Cavalry, was captured in Hanover, Pennsylvania, on June 30, 1863. Arriving at Fort Delaware on July 7, 1863, Sergeant French was among the first prisoners to occupy the newly built barracks. French was from Stafford Courthouse, Virginia, and a schoolteacher both before and after the war. (Fort Delaware Society.)

Two Columbiad guns protect the northwest bastion in this 1863 image, part of a rare Fort Delaware stereograph. The staff officer quarters can be seen in the distance immediately above the gun. The far right building was the engineer and surgeon quarters. (Delaware Historical Society.)

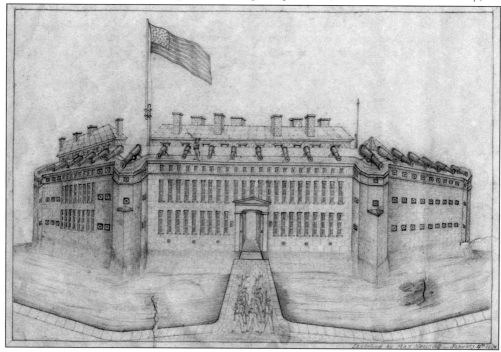

Pvt. Max Neugas of the Pee Dee Light Artillery sketched Fort Delaware on January 4, 1864. Neugas, a Jewish emigrant from Baden, was captured at Gettysburg. While a prisoner, he drew over a dozen scenes documenting life on the island. (Fort Delaware Society.)

Max Neugas's April 18, 1864, northeast bastion sketch is near perfect. The gun is a 10-inch Columbiad mounted on a barbette carriage. (Fort Delaware Society.)

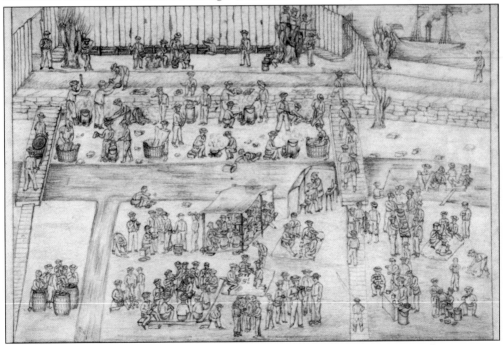

Max Neugas sketched this rendition of the prison exercise yard in 1864. "I got the pan, went where they were cooking, and found several hundred prisoners, many of them cooking. They had made little holes in the ground, or set up bricks, over which they set their pots and pans. The cut pieces of plank, shingles etc into shavings with which they kept up a blaze. . . . Some of them were making a sort of soup, by boiling their bread, some who had money or tobacco were making coffee or tea, frying fish, beef, etc. or boiling vegetables," according to Capt. John S. Swann, 26th Virginia Infantry. (Fort Delaware Society.)

In mid-1864, a group of soldiers and civilians gathers outside of the prison guardhouse. From left to right are (sitting) two unidentified civilians, John Welch (sutler), Lt. Abraham G. Wolf (assistant commissary of prisoners), Lt. Charles Hawkins (provost marshal), and Allen H. Conlon (hospital steward); (standing) unidentified, Pvt. W. H. Depue, Pvt. William W. Randolph, Pvt. James H. Hoyt, Sgt. George Miller, Pvt. Robert McPherson, Cpl. Guy Cunningham, and Capt. Stanislaus Mlotkowski. Note "Bill the Cat" by Lt. Wolf's feet. (Photograph by John L. Gihon, courtesy of Fort Delaware Society.)

On July 30, 1864, inside the prison guardhouse, Lt. Abraham Wolf's clerks go about business as usual. This rare interior view, sketched by Max Neugas, provides a glimpse of a 19th-century office. An artist (likely Neugas) is sketching by the window, while "Bill the Cat" is relaxing in the background. (Fort Delaware Society.)

"Considerable stir with our crowd preparing to have picture taken. Have mine taken, order half doz. John L. Gihon, Photographic Art Galleries, 1024 Chestnut Street, Philadelphia, PA, is the artist. Paid $2.50 dollars to the artist," stated Col. William W. Ward, 9th Tennessee Cavalry, on April 23, 1864. (Fort Delaware Society.)

This 1864 Gihon image shows Union soldiers and at least one Confederate at an unverified location on the island. A guard shack on the extreme right, covered with gum blankets or like material, possibly doubled as Gihon's dark room. Nineteenth-century wet-plate photography would require immediate on-site processing. The glass negatives would be useless once dry, hence the term wet-plate. (Fort Delaware Society.)

The Confederate barracks, post hospital, icehouse, and guardhouse (with flag) appear in this 1864 bird's-eye sketch. The "Government Farm" in New Jersey (a Confederate burial site) and the steamer *Osceola* are in the upper right. (Sketch by Max Neugas, courtesy of Boston Athenaeum.)

Reverend Handy said that Pvt. Bailey Peyton Key of the 14th Tennessee Cavalry "is the only person, save one, of his entire company who has not taken the oath of allegiance to the Yankee Government. Among those who have thus proved recreant to the cause, are his two brothers. In reply to a letter from his mother, urging him to follow the example of his brothers, the lad wrote that he would 'die first.' He is an intelligent youth, and a hero of many battles." Key was only 14 years old when photographed in 1864. After the war, Key graduated from the University of Nashville (1874) and received further medical training at Jefferson College in Philadelphia. On June 28, 1913, Bailey Peyton Key, M.D. died of pneumonia. He was 63 years old. (Photograph by John L. Gihon, courtesy of Fort Delaware Society.)

Lt. Washington L. Watkins, 8th Missouri Cavalry, arrived in late March 1864 with another 270 Confederate officers. As with several other Gihon images, Watkins poses with an officer sword, belt, sash, and other accoutrements. These props are likely the property of Lt. William Hall, from Battery G. (Delaware State Parks.)

"We formed in line and marched to the mess hall, in which were several long rows of plank tables with pieces of bread and meat arranged along the sides at intervals of some two feet. When we were in place each prisoner took one ration," explained Capt. John S. Swann, 26th Virginia Infantry. (Sketch by Max Neugas, courtesy of Fort Delaware Society.)

John Gihon visited the prison barracks for this April 29, 1864, photograph. From left to right are (seated) Maj. William G. Bullitt, Capt. Ralph Sheldon, Capt. Samuel Taylor, Capt. E. W. McLean, and Lt. Thomas W. Bullitt; (standing) Capt. J. H. Hamby, Capt. H. C. Meriwether, Maj. Thomas Webber (with sword), Capt. R. D. Logan, Maj. Lamar Fontaine, Lt. Anderson Berry, and Capt. J. S. Chapman. (Filson Historical Society.)

In this woodcut, Handy poses with members of his theological class. Seated from left to right are Lt. J. N. McFarland, Capt. G. L. Roberts, and Capt. W. F. Gordon; (standing) Rev. Isaac W. K. Handy, Capt. J. H. Dye, Lt. Wash C. Shane, Lt. T. S. Armistead, Capt. J. J. Dunkle, and Lt. J. T. Mackey. (Delaware State Parks.)

Lt. Miles Izates Taylor, Company H, 26th Alabama Infantry, commanded his entire regiment through attrition at Chancellorsville. Lieutenant Taylor was wounded at Gettysburg and captured on July 5, 1863. At Fort Delaware, Taylor occupied "the same apartment with the surgeons, lately removed into the Fort." He was transferred to Johnson's Island in November of the same year. In 1865, he was sent to Point Lookout, then back to Fort Delaware for exchange. After the war, Taylor moved to Texas, marrying Laura Alice Hindman. (Courtesy of Ruth Anderton, great-granddaughter.)

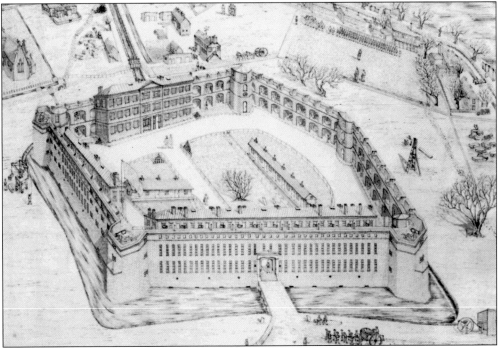

On March 6, 1864, Handy noted that "the yellow framed building, immediately in front of our quarters, occupied by Company Q, took fire this afternoon, and for about fifteen minutes created an intense excitement." Hamilton further observed that "they were inside the fort and the fire was likely to do some damage. Fortunately we succeeded in extinguishing it." Schoepf later requested "Having the frame buildings inside the fort removed, as they were at one time on fire and liable to catch on fire at any time again, and from their close proximity to the magazines thereby greatly endanger the safety of the fort." (Sketch by Max Neugas, courtesy of Boston Athenaeum.)

On September 12, 1863, Private Hamilton wrote that "the men were all drawn up to witness the dedication of the laying of the cornerstone of our new church. The scene was quite impressive." On May 2, 1864, Reverend Handy noted "A man named Stevens, belonging to Battery A . . . detailed as painter on the new church, fell down the stairs in one of the towers, some time last night, and was killed." (Author's collection.)

Prisoners and soldiers alike could purchase goods from the sutler, who usually sold at exorbitant prices. Sutler John Welch, seated in middle group, was one such merchant who did business on the island. (Photograph by John L. Gihon, courtesy of Fort Delaware Society.)

Col. Basil W. Duke of Kentucky was second-in-command to his brother-in-law Gen. John Hunt Morgan. A Major Johnson escorted Duke, now a prisoner, on the train to Fort Delaware. Johnson shared "a flask of excellent brandy, a package of sandwiches and cigars," and allowed Duke to share a room with him at the Continental Hotel in Philadelphia prior to his arrival at Pea Patch. Johnson was under fire later for his friendliness. Handy described Duke as "a young man of about 30 years, very gentlemanly in his manners, and fluent in conversation." He was "about 5 feet 10 inches in height, of dark complexion, and wears a brown goatee and light moustache. He has a small, keen, chestnut eye, pleasing face, and good teeth. His forehead, which is low, is overhung with heavy eye-brows. He has been three times wounded in the service of his country." (Photograph by John L. Gihon, courtesy of Fort Delaware Society.)

The Morgan brothers, Col. Richard "Dick" Morgan (left) and Capt. Charlton Morgan, were the younger brothers of the infamous John Hunt Morgan, known for his Ohio raids. Col. Dick Morgan was a prisoner at Fort Delaware twice. (Photographs by John L. Gihon, courtesy of Fort Delaware Society.)

On April 30, 1864, Rev. Isaac Handy sits in "the central position, with General Vance on the right, and Gen. Thompson on the left—the others seated on either side, or standing in the rear, with Bailey Key, the orderly, on a blanket in front. Something was said about bringing a couple of Rebel ladies into the picture. Gen. Jeff [Thompson]. Good-humoredly suggested that it was 'bad enough to introduce a *preacher* into such company; and so the ladies, beautiful, and thoroughly 'secesh,' will be more appropriately daguerreotyped upon the heart of certain distinguished heroes, for whom their visit was more especially intended," as Handy wrote in his diary. (Photograph by John L. Gihon, courtesy of Fort Delaware Society.)

Handy wrote that Brig. Gen. Robert Vance "has a modest blue eye and a staid, settled visage, with an occasional smile, showing a good set of teeth, under his long brown moustache. His frame is rather muscular, his height medium, and he is a rapid walker, stooping slightly forward as he moves." After the war, Vance ended up working with Schoepf at the U.S. Patent Office. (Photograph by John L. Gihon, courtesy of Fort Delaware Society.)

From left to right are (seated) Morgan Jenkins, Joseph Boyd, Lt. Abraham G. Wolf, George Fleming, Cpl. John Newland, and John Fitzsimmons; (standing) William Calhoun, William Hardwick, Cpl. Emanuel M. Cockley, and Hampden McCreary. "Marg. Fleming, New Brighton, PA" is handwritten on the back of this photograph. (Photograph by John L. Gihon, author's collection.)

Lt. Henry Warner took over as post adjutant following Lt. John G. MacConnell's return to company duty. Warner, from Battery G, is seated in the center. (Photograph by John L. Gihon, courtesy of Gilder Lehrman Institute.)

Lt. Alfred Herr, center, stands with other Battery G soldiers for this 1864 Gihon albumen. On April 10, 1865, Private Hamilton wrote, "At noon a salute of 225 guns was fired with Lt. Herr commanding." (Gilder Lehrman Institute.)

From left to right are (seated) Cpl. James O'Neil, Thomas Crooks, John Chambers, William Humphreys, and John Campbell; (standing) Harvey B. Chess, John McCutcheon, James Eccles, Sgt. Walter Chess, Lt. Alfred Herr, John Lorentz, William Young, and Cpl. Andrew Bryce. All are members of Young's Battery. (Photograph by John L. Gihon, courtesy of Gilder Lehrman Institute.)

Cpl. Guy Cunningham of Allegheny County, Pennsylvania, sits in the immediate center of Battery G members. The officer to Cunningham's left is Lt. William Hall. The officer standing at center is Lt. Frank W. Hay. Cunningham worked as an acting hospital steward during the war. (Photograph by John L. Gihon, courtesy of Gilder Lehrman Institute.)

Private Hamilton's battery, originally classified as heavy artillery, made a change to light artillery, as evidenced by this photograph. "We had to make a trip to No. 3 Wharf for a box of clothing said to be light artillery uniforms for us. Boys are a good deal excited about it and swear they will not have them. Officers are anxious to effect the change which will increase their own pay from $15 to $20 a month. . . . That evening in quarters I found the boys in a great rage over the light artillery question. Most of them swore to go under arrest rather than submit to the change." (Photograph by John L. Gihon, courtesy of Gilder Lehrman Institute.)

The 6th Massachusetts Infantry arrived on August 23, 1864, by the steamer *Major Reybold*, replacing the 157th Ohio Infantry. Capt. Edgar J. Sherman (left) commanded Company K of the 6th. The *Lawrence American* described Sherman as "no braver or more faithful officer . . . always attentive to the needs of his men." Sherman, a veteran soldier, saw combat with the 48th Massachusetts at Port Hudson. (Fort Delaware Society.)

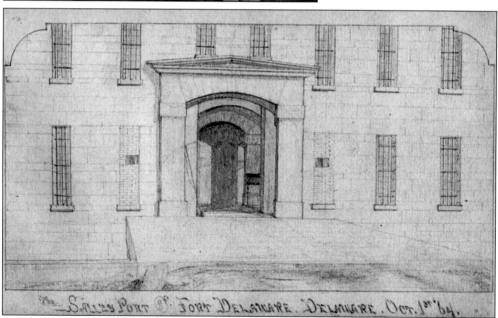

Pvt. Baldwin Coolidge, from Capt. Edgar Sherman's Company K, worked on a portfolio of sketches during his tenure at Fort Delaware. Coolidge (1845–1928) went on to be a well-known and respected New England photographer, credited with contributing to the creation of Modernism. (Delaware Historical Society.)

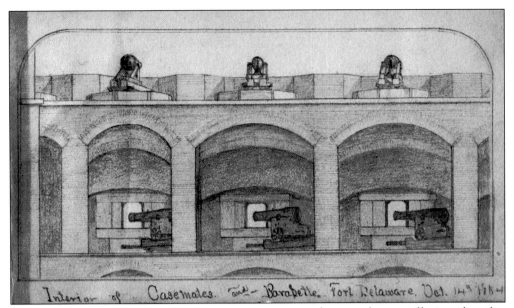

Interior of Casemates and Barbette. Fort Delaware. Oct. 14th 1864

The second-tier casemates and barbette gun mounts on the terreplein are illustrated in this Coolidge sketch. The fort was armed with a combination of 32-pounder seacoast guns, 8- and 10-inch Columbiads, 8- and 10-inch Rodmans, and 24-pounder flank howitzers. Records also indicate that the island had a complement of six field pieces. (Delaware Historical Society.)

On September 26, 1864, the 165th New York Infantry (2nd Battalion Duryee's Zouaves) sent "75 more men to take prisoners to Fort Delaware." Baldwin Coolidge's sketch documents their visit, showing the elaborate Zouave attire of an unknown corporal. (Delaware Historical Society.)

A daguerreotype of Gilbert Clark's children was the centerpiece on a brooch worn by Ellen Clark all her life. Ellen Amanda, on the far left, lived on the island for a time with her father; the other two children passed away before the war, and his first wife died in 1862. Ellen reportedly attended a "Young Ladies School" in Salem, New Jersey, on weekdays. (Fort Delaware Society.)

An 1860s history of the 6th Massachusetts Infantry recorded that "Fort Delaware is a fine fortification, on Pea-Patch Island, about midway between the New Jersey and Delaware Shores, some forty miles below Philadelphia, in the Delaware River." (Sketch by Baldwin Coolidge, courtesy of Delaware Historical Society.)

On April 16, 1865, following Lincoln's assassination, the 165th New York Infantry "took train for Wilmington, thence to New Castle. We caused considerable commotion, as the people never before had seen a Zouave regiment. Citizens very kind to us, providing us with supper; left by boat late at night for Fort Delaware," according to an 1870s history of the regiment. The New York Zouaves were brought there to quell any potential prisoner uprising relating to Lincoln's death. (The Military and Historical Image Bank.)

John L. Gihon continued to capture photographic images of civilians, soldiers, and prisoners, as well as structures on the island, until the late 1860s. He was a baseball card pioneer, creating several designs for the Philadelphia Athletics in the 1870s. In 1876, Gihon was a feature photographer at the Centennial Exhibition in Philadelphia. In 1878, he published the *Photographic Colorists' Guide*, which emphasized his multum in parvo ideals. On September 16, 1878, while returning from Venezuela due to illness, Gihon died at sea. He was 39 years old. (Author's collection.)

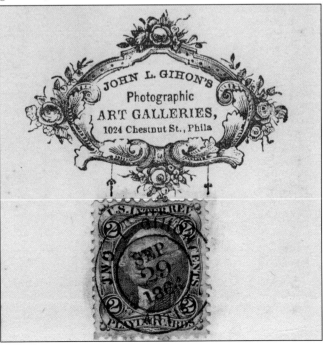

Two unidentified soldiers, one Confederate, one Union, had their photographs taken at the end of the war. The majority of prisoners were released by June 27, 1865, along with discharge of the garrison. (Photographs by John L. Gihon, author's collection.)

Bernard B. Graves was one of the last Confederates to be sent to Fort Delaware. Graves, a member of the Virginia Amherst Light Artillery, was captured in Waynesboro, Virginia, in March 1865. Military records indicate Graves was 5 feet, 9 inches tall, with blue eyes, dark hair, and a fair complexion. (Photograph by Rees and Brothers, courtesy of the Library of Congress.)

# *Three*

# MODERNIZATION OF FORT DELAWARE 1866–1900

When the last prisoner left Fort Delaware, the post reverted to being protector of the Delaware. Extensive repair of buildings, embankment walls, and docks utilized the remaining fort treasury of $46,000. However, the Columbiad smoothbore guns could only fire about a mile; by 1870, the structure was essentially obsolete. A test fire aimed directly at a southern face of the fort resulted in extensive damage. With the advent of updated ordnance, masonry forts rapidly became a thing of the past. Fifteen-inch Rodman guns were added to the installation between 1870 and 1875.

The fort was never garrisoned again to the previous extent. Piles of cannonballs sit gathering dust in an image. By 1870, the garrison was withdrawn, and the U.S. Army Corps of Engineers took over the post. An 1878 storm with 70-mile-per-hour winds caused extensive damage to the island. According to Col. J. N. Macomb of the corps, "many of the people living in the island barely escaped with their lives." An 1884 article in the *Wilmington Morning News* painted a picture of the island:

> The island within the banks includes about 90 acres and three families live upon it outside the fort. They all keep cows and have garden and corn patches. Most of the outside buildings, except for three houses, are rapidly going in to decay. . . . The old chapel is now used for the storage of hay. The barracks occupied by the rebel prisoners during the war have all disappeared and their former site is occupied by pasture land and corn fields. . . . The population of the island included in the six families (three within the fort walls) is about 20. Patrick McHugh who lives in the north building inside the fort, has been there for 36 years, while Patrick Gunning has lived there for 33 years.

But the government was reluctant to let go of its investment. In 1890, a congressional committee evaluated the condition of coastal defenses, and Fort Delaware's renaissance began. In 1892, a mine control casemate was built, followed by the construction of a three-gun lift battery, which included 12-inch disappearing guns with a range of 8 miles. Rapid-fire gun batteries were added. By 1900, Fort Delaware was officially part of a coastal defense system that included Fort DuPont in Delaware City and Fort Mott in New Jersey.

This Gihon and Jones image was taken after the war; the soldiers in the photograph are from the 4th U.S. Artillery. Two companies of the 4th inconsistently garrisoned the fort until the late 1890s. (Delaware Historical Society.)

An 1860s history of the 6th Massachusetts Infantry recorded that "A gem of Gothic architecture had been erected by Gen. Schoepf, to conserve the religious interest of those who should be stationed at the post; and the chapel was regularly open on the Sabbath twice." Soldiers and hoop-skirted women stand near the chapel's entrance. The structure was severely damaged by a storm in 1878 and then used as a hay barn. The chapel was completely demolished in 1902. (Photograph by Gihon and Jones, courtesy of Fort Delaware Society.)

A view looking north shows the back of the fort, compete with postern and footbridge. The moat is now drained, and a large Rodman gun tube waits to be mounted. Note the shadow in the front of the photograph, likely that of John L. Gihon. (Delaware Historical Society.)

Columbiads and Rodmans line the third tier (front II) in this postwar Fort Delaware image. (Photograph by Gihon and Jones, Delaware Historical Society.)

Between 1867 and 1868, the engineers prepared the casemate embrasure for a test fire. Due to the advancement in weaponry, the U.S. Department of War wanted to test the structure. The embrasure's test plate, a 15-inch-thick iron shield, is shown above. (Delaware Historical Society.)

Test firing took place from a distance of 120 yards in December 1868. Projectiles were fired at the embrasure from a 15-inch Rodman and a 12-inch ordnance rifle. (Delaware Historical Society.)

The result of the test firing was devastating to the embrasure. Two steel and five cast iron cannonballs as well as one shell were fired, tearing apart not only the iron plate but also the surrounding masonry. (Delaware Historical Society.)

The final damage filled the casemate (number 17, front II) with debris and shrapnel that would have killed any gunners inside. The U.S. Department of War shifted focus to defensive earthworks as a safer alternative than confined masonry casemates. (Delaware Historical Society.)

The east side of Pea Patch Island shows a few buildings, the sluiceway, and the 1870s modernization of Fort Delaware's bastions. (Delaware State Parks.)

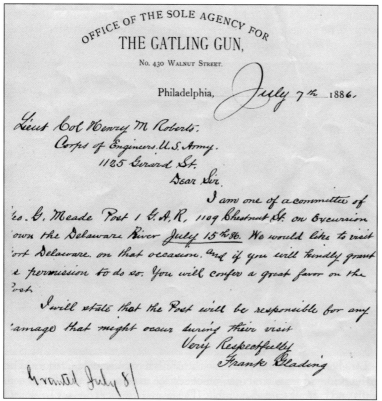

Even in 1886, Fort Delaware was a tourist destination. The George G. Meade GAR post requests a visit in this July 7 letter. Sightseeing visits to the island are documented as early as the 1820s. (Delaware State Parks.)

*Casemate, Peapatch Island – Looking Southeastward (Under Construction Sept. 6 – 1892)*

In 1892, a mine control casemate was constructed on the north end of island, near the site of the former cemetery and smallpox hospital. The controlled submarine mines were watertight steel cases strategically placed in the river. They contained explosive and firing devices with means of electrical detonation from the shore. An earlier 1874 plan for a mine control casemate never materialized. (Fort Delaware Society.)

Progress continues above on the mine control casemate. Following construction, the station housed the power and control equipment necessary for operation of the mines. U.S. Department of War policy stated that controlled mines were limited to distances not exceeding 10,000 yards from shore and to depths not greater than 250 feet. The number of mines and planting depth was dependent upon the locality to be defended. (Fort Delaware Society.)

Construction continues on the mine control casemate in this 1892 photograph. Besides the mine control casemate, a torpedo storehouse was constructed in 1897 (near the damaged chapel) and a system of tramway tracks was built on the island. The tramway tracks ran between the torpedo storehouse, the interior of the fort, and the wharf. (Fort Delaware Society.)

Men stationed in the bombproof rooms operated the electrical signals that detonated the minefield during an engagement. Empty mines were stored inside the fort, and materials were stored in the torpedo warehouse outside the fort. (Fort Delaware Society.)

In 1892, workers put finishing touches by covering the control casemate with soil. The natural camouflage, paired with the bomb-proof casemate, would protect soldiers during an engagement. The concealment is still effective today, due to the natural growth of foliage. (Fort Delaware Society.)

In the same year as the mine control casemate construction, visits to the island by civilians continued. On June 6, 1892, permission is granted for the Sängerbund to visit Fort Delaware. The same year, "visitors—accidental drowning" is included in the official engineer report. (Delaware State Parks.)

INFANTRY UNIT—B (FORT DELAWARE) FRESH FROM CUBA 1898
FIRST DIVISION U.S. ARMY

The Spanish-American War inspired the government to reevaluate coastal and harbor defenses, embarking on a large-scale modernization movement. Above, 1st Division "Infantry Unit B" troops are photographed. On May 30, 1898, "The island at present is a swamp owing to the abandonment and neglect for over twenty-five years. . . . The casemate quarters, with the exception of those now occupied by Battery L, 4th Artillery, have been knocked out by the Engineers preparatory to the construction of a 12 inch Rifle Battery," stated Maj. Van Arsdale Andruss. (Fort Delaware Society.)

In 1898, workers are seen during construction of a rapid-fire battery on Pea Patch Island. The emplacement, later named Battery Dodd, was home for two 4.72-inch British rapid-fire guns. Note the mortar and stack of projectiles in the upper right corner. (Delaware Public Archives.)

Another view, looking northeast, shows Battery Dodd from top of the riverbank. One of Dodd's gun foundations is seen in the foreground, with complimenting magazines to the left and right. Construction occurred from June 22, 1898, until December 1, 1898. (Delaware Public Archives.)

In another northeast view, around 1898, construction continues with the additional buildup of the magazines. (Delaware Public Archives.)

Construction workers take a break in this 1898 photograph. The rapid-fire battery's primary mission was to protect the mine control casemate and minefield. Cover fire for the interior batteries could also be provided. (Delaware Public Archives.)

Finishing touches are made on the top pavement of the battery as the project nears completion. The photographer is strategically positioned on a crane for this 1898 image. (Delaware Public Archives.)

The completed rapid-fire battery is seen from Fort Delaware's southwest bastion. In the foreground, duel magazine entrances are seen at the base of the battery. Battery Dodd is named in honor of a Civil War soldier, Capt. Albert Dodd of the 17th U.S. Infantry, who was killed on June 27, 1862, at the Battle of Gaines Mill, Virginia. (Delaware Public Archives.)

On April 29, 1898, Capt. William Corrett reported "that two 4.724-inch Armstrong Rapid fire guns will be mounted and ready for firing by tomorrow, or the next day." In c. 1898 photograph, the Armstrong guns can be seen mounted on the ramparts. The same year, the guns would be removed and remounted on Battery Dodd. (Delaware Public Archives.)

A photographer stands in the third-floor window of the brick officer quarters to capture this photograph of the three-gun battery construction inside the fort. The new battery, later known as Torbert, would house three 12-inch guns on disappearing carriages. To make room for Battery Torbert, half of the brick soldier barracks and a set of officer quarters were torn down. (Delaware Public Archives.)

Another image shows further construction of the three-gun battery. Most batteries built during the 1890s only had two levels, but Battery Torbert would have three. (Delaware Public Archives.)

The 15-inch Rodman magazines are being demolished in this 1899 photograph. The magazines' rubble was used to fill the sand core of the three-gun battery. (Delaware Public Archives.)

The room on the right (crane on top) is the battery's power station. It was home for three General Electric Model GM-12 generators. (Delaware Public Archives.)

Construction of Battery Torbert's first-floor corridors can be seen in this 1899 photograph. The rooms were used to house equipment related to the ordnance detail. (Delaware Public Archives.)

This western view shows ongoing construction of the second tier. Filling of the sand core continues in the background, along with the rubble from the 1870s magazines. (Delaware Public Archives.)

Back in 1894, Maj. Charles W. Raymond and Lt. Spencer Cosby initially planned the 12-inch gun battery to serve as a gun lift battery. By 1896, construction halted due to newly invented disappearing gun carriages. The gun lift battery plans were scrapped for the more favorable design to support disappearing gun carriages. Construction resumed in August 1897 and lasted until late 1899. (Delaware Public Archives.)

Battery Torbert was named after army officer Gen. Alfred Torbert, a Delaware native born in Georgetown. A Civil War veteran, he drowned in August 1880 after the sinking of the SS *Vera Cruz*. Reportedly, he swam for over 20 hours before dying on the shore of Cape Canaveral, Florida. General Torbert is buried in the Methodist Episcopal Cemetery in Milford, Delaware. (Delaware Public Archives.)

Battery Dodd can be seen outside of the fort in the background. The two pits to the right of the photograph are for the 3-inch rapid-fire guns, later named Battery Allen. Lt. Robert Allen Jr., 1st U.S. Cavalry, died during the Peninsula Campaign of 1862. (Delaware Public Archives.)

In 1899, asphalting of the third floor of the service platform level is in progress. The asphalt was later removed because the shot carts, laden with heavy projectiles, wound sink into the material. (Delaware Public Archives.)

In 1900, a 12-inch gun is positioned on the top of the three-gun battery. The guns were so large that an extra concrete platform, running the entire length of the battery, was later added. (Delaware Public Archives.)

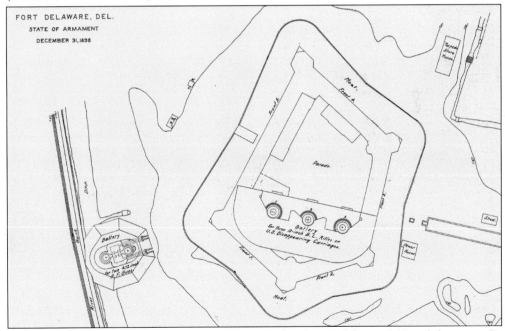

FORT DELAWARE, DEL.
STATE OF ARMAMENT
DECEMBER 31, 1898

The official armament plan indicates the locations for the rapid-fire and 12-inch batteries. By 1900, these batteries were manned by Battery L of the 4th U.S. Artillery. The following year, the unit was redesignated as the 45th Company, Coast Artillery Corps. (National Archives.)

Two of Torbert's 12-inch guns are shown in the firing position. When fired, they would recoil in the lower loading position. Mounted on disappearing carriages, they were lifted via counterweights above the wall when ready to fire. (Delaware Historical Society.)

Two of the power station's three General Electric Model GM-12 generators appear in this undated photograph. It was critical that coastal fortifications provided their own power. Fort Delaware continued to generate her own power via generators well into the 21st century. (Fort Delaware Society.)

# Four

# WORLDWIDE WARFARE 1901–1945

With the military back in command, artillery units arrived in late 1901. Coastal Artillery units including the 112th (based at mainland Fort DuPont) and the 119th (Fort Mott in New Jersey) marked a change in strategy focusing more on mainland fortifications. By 1902, the headquarters for harbor and river defense was designated as Fort DuPont, moving Fort Delaware into a lesser role with no permanent garrison. By 1904, the artillery detachment was once again pulled from Fort Delaware, and the Army Corps of Engineers returned.

The government worked to raise the island's level using dredging spoils from the new 30-foot channel in the river. This effort to stem tidal and flood damage was also aimed at protecting the upgraded artillery. Dike walls were raised, and alterations were made to the structures such as batteries Hentig and Dodd so that the entrances would not be covered by spoils. Spoils were permitted to settle until 1912. However, overgrowth was getting out of control. The assistant engineer commented on the problem:

> If practicable, the reservation at Fort Delaware, recently filled with dredging material, be leased, under suitable restrictions, for cultivation during the coming summer. . . . Willow sprouts and brush of different kinds are taking root and spreading fast and unless checked by cultivation will be difficult to eradicate. The whole area is also covered with a rank growth of weeds from 3 to 6 feet high during the summer, in which mosquitoes and sheep flies are so thick that living on the island is very uncomfortable.

World War I brought with it a reinforcement of the post. From February 1917 to December 1918, the 3rd Company, Coast Artillery came from Fort DuPont to garrison the island. Upon war's end, the force was reduced to only four men. From here on, Fort Delaware was essentially an outpost of Fort DuPont. Island duty was to "warn off trespassers, to paint mines and equipment, and to care for the modern guns."

World War II marked a new chapter in the fort's history. Battery C, 261st Coast Artillery, a Delaware National Guard unit, garrisoned the island behind the strength of Battery Hentig's two 3-inch guns. Once the southern harbor defense of Fort Miles, located at Cape Henlopen in Lewes, was completed, Fort Delaware was no longer needed. The garrison returned to Fort DuPont, and Fort Delaware was once again army surplus by 1945.

A photographer took a picture of two soldiers manning one of the 3-inch batteries constructed on top of Battery Torbert. Batteries Allen and Albertus each had a complement of two 3-inch guns, flanking Battery Torbert. The guns had a range of 4.5 miles. (Delaware State Parks.)

Battery Torbert's shot hoist, a projectile elevator, was used to transport the heavy rounds to Fort Delaware's third level. Batteries Torbert, Dodd, Allen, Albertus, and Hentig (next to Dodd) were officially named by General Order No. 78, dated May 25, 1903. (Delaware State Parks.)

In March 1919, Pvt. James C. Davis of the Coast Artillery Corps was "sent over to Ft. Delaware with orders to clear out everything except the disappearing rifles. We were not to dump anything in the river nor to bring it back to the mainland." A Wisconsin native, Davis provided valuable information and photographs from this time period. (Delaware State Parks.)

A real photo postcard shows the interior of James Davis's home office inside Fort Delaware. (Photograph by James C. Davis, courtesy of Delaware State Parks.)

An unidentified soldier sits atop one of the 12-inch guns; Pvt. James Davis stands next to the piece. The 1895-model 12-inch gun weighed 114,700 pounds. According to the U.S. Army Technical Manual, it had a maximum range of 13,500 yards, or about 8 miles. (Delaware State Parks.)

A view from Battery Torbert facing northwest shows the soldier barracks on the left and the remaining set of officer quarters on the right. The set of officer quarters demolished in the 1890s would be to the photographer's far right. (Delaware State Parks.)

Pvt. James Davis poses with mines in Fort Delaware's parade grounds. The mine components consisted of the maneuvering ring (seen on top), the mine case, and the center rim. The mine's blasting cap was located on the underside. (Delaware State Parks.)

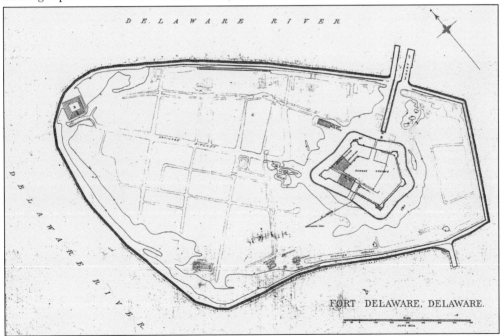

A 1904 map shows early elevations on Pea Patch Island. The same year, 5 to 10 feet of dredge spoil was deposited on the island, drastically changing the island's acreage and level. The 1890s mine control casemate can be seen on the north end (left) of the island. In 1919, Private Davis wrote, "we would load up this barge, push it along into the sloughs as far as it would go and then just roll the stuff over the side into the mud." (Delaware State Parks.)

A local church group visits the island in September 1932. Note the tramway tracks in foreground. (Fort Delaware Society.)

A 1930s interior view of the fort shows enclosed casemates. Decades earlier, on January 8, 1903, Captain Campbell, post commander, requested "authority to enclose three casemates of the old fort at this Post in such manner as to make them suitable for use [as a] guard house and prison cell." The "General Prisoners" were most likely military convicts, including deserters. (Fort Delaware Society.)

In the 1930s, Fort Delaware was officially designated as a sub-post of Fort DuPont, located on the mainland in Delaware City. Fort DuPont originated in 1864 as the Ten-Gun Battery, an auxiliary to Fort Delaware during the Civil War. (Author's collection.)

Pfc. William M. Thomas (right) of Company D, First Engineers, was stationed at Fort DuPont from 1934 to 1936. During this time period, Fort DuPont was primarily an engineer post, with only a small coastal artillery force. (Barry Thomas.)

Pfc. William M. Thomas took this snapshot of engineers by one of Battery Torbert's 12-inch guns. To the left is one of the three stairwell tower caps for the three-gun lift. During the 1930s, Fort DuPont soldiers often made leisure trips to the island. These soldiers regularly took photographs and even fort relics as mementoes. In 1930, an original "100-year-old oak and bronze" powder magazine door was acquired by Capt. William R. Maris, then commanding officer of Fort DuPont. (Barry Thomas.)

First Engineer soldiers clad in bathing suits climb on a 3-inch gun belonging to Battery Hentig. The majority of soldier snapshots from this era show relaxation and downtime at Fort Delaware. Hentig's guns were transferred to Fort Miles during World War II. (Barry Thomas.)

A 12-inch gun complete with disappearing carriage is shown in the firing position. Disappearing carriages only had a limited angle of elevation, making the guns effective against flat-trajectory naval fire. The guns were obsolete with the onset of aviation warfare and long-range naval guns. (Photograph by William M. Thomas, courtesy of Barry Thomas.)

Thomas's photograph of the east side of Fort Delaware shows the tramway bridge, which replaced the original version for foot traffic. During the Civil War, this side of the fort was the first thing seen by Confederate prisoners upon their arrival on Pea Patch Island. (Barry Thomas.)

CONFIDENTIAL

V-4-86IF-97X(9-3-40-II.55A)(8.25-2500) FORT DELAWARE, DELAWARE

In March 1940, army aerial photographs show Torbert's three guns still mounted. The rapid-fire guns in Batteries Allen and Albertus were disarmed during the 1920s. In November 1940, the 12-inch gun tubes were removed and remounted at Fort Amezquita, Puerto Rico. (Delaware State Parks.)

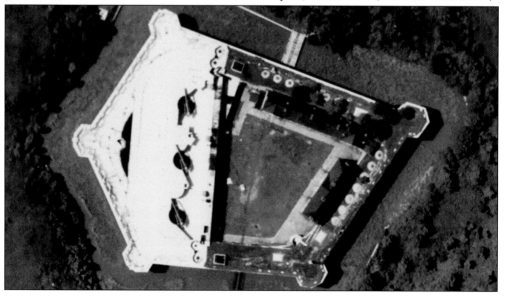

An undated photograph of the fort's interior shows the enlisted barracks, the tramway with car, and the Delaware shoreline in the distance. During World War II, the post was garrisoned by a detachment of Battery C, 261st Coast Artillery, a Delaware National Guard unit. (Delaware State Parks.)

A coast artillery soldier, clad in his army denims, breaks regulations by opting for a more comfortable pair of civilian shoes. (Photograph by Joseph Corti, courtesy of Delaware State Parks.)

A playful moment on the parapet involves a 1903 Springfield rifle complete with bayonet. The aggressor sports an early 1940s helmet similar to that worn in World War I. (Photograph by Joseph Corti, courtesy of Delaware State Parks.)

This eastern view on the ramparts shows the Jersey shoreline in the distance. A surfaced submarine can also be seen. (Photograph by Joseph Corti, courtesy of Delaware State Parks.)

This 1942 photograph shows one of Battery Torbert's disappearing carriages in the loading position minus the gun. The guns, removed in November 1940, were followed by the removal of the carriages. The carriages were scrapped in March 1943. (Photograph by Joseph Corti, courtesy of Delaware State Parks.)

Col. George Ruhlen, second from right, gives a tour of Fort Delaware in 1941. Colonel Ruhlen commanded the Harbor Defenses on the Delaware, which included Forts Delaware, Mott, DuPont, Saulsbury, and Miles. Gov. Walter Bacon stands second from the left. (Delaware State Parks.)

In 1942, Sgt. William A. Smith (standing) and Cpl. John H. Prettyman, both members of Battery C, 261st Coast Artillery, enjoy their time at Fort Delaware. (Delaware Military Heritage and Education Foundation.)

A 1940s interior view of the fort shows the overhang added to Battery Torbert in 1910. Engineers failed to plan adequately for space needed to work on the massive size of the guns in the loading position. (Delaware State Parks.)

Pvt. Norman Willin, Battery C, 261st Coast Artillery, practices the manual of arms on the ramparts of Fort Delaware around 1942. (Photograph by William Smith, courtesy of Delaware Military Heritage and Education Foundation.)

A 1942 snapshot shows the area once occupied by a set of brick officer quarters. The closed casemates and a remaining 1870s magazine also survive. (Photograph by Joseph Corti, courtesy of Delaware State Parks.)

This snapshot states on the reverse side, "View looking west, north face." Near the farthest barbette mount, a Rodman gun tube peeks out from a mound of dirt. (Photograph by George Ruhlen, courtesy of Fort Delaware Society.)

A close-up shot of the 15-inch Rodman, buried in the parapet, along the bastion where it was once mounted. Rather than moving or shipping it elsewhere, the gun was just quickly covered. (Delaware Public Archives.)

Colonel Ruhlen ordered the gun exhumed and examined. After the gun was determined to be unloaded, it was Fort Delaware's contribution to the scrap metal drive. Guns were also scrapped at nearby Fort Mott in New Jersey. In May 1944, the *Fort DuPont Flashes*, a post publication, reported, "Outmoded seacoast artillery at Forts Delaware and Mott have been cut up and hauled away as scrap. The metal (steel barrels and mounts and lead counterweights) will be used to aid our war effort. Samuels & Sons, contractors, were the high bidders and paid the Government a lump sum for the privilege of breaking up and taking away the metal for sale to steel mills for the production of weapons." (Fort Delaware Society.)

A worker cuts into the Rodman with an oxyacetylene torch, which was a fate shared by many other similar relics during World War II. The generator room, parade grounds, and a couple of remaining shutters complete the backdrop of this 1944 snapshot. (Delaware State Parks.)

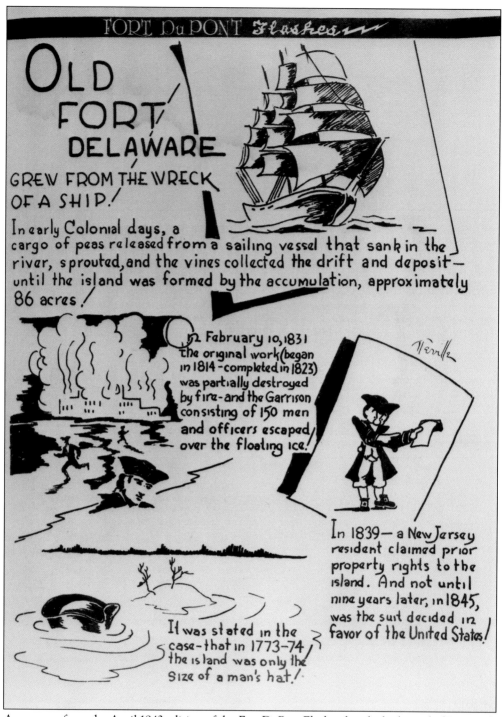

# OLD FORT DELAWARE

## GREW FROM THE WRECK OF A SHIP!

In early Colonial days, a cargo of peas released from a sailing vessel that sank in the river, sprouted, and the vines collected the drift and deposit— until the island was formed by the accumulation, approximately 86 acres.

On February 10, 1831 the original work (began in 1814 - completed in 1823) was partially destroyed by fire - and the Garrison consisting of 150 men and officers escaped over the floating ice!

In 1839— a New Jersey resident claimed prior property rights to the island. And not until nine years later, in 1845, was the suit decided in favor of the United States!

It was stated in the case - that in 1773-74 the island was only the size of a man's hat!

An excerpt from the April 1943 edition of the *Fort DuPont Flashes* details the legend of Pea Patch Island. While many facts and figures stray from the truth, the basic story line is sound. (Artwork by Pvt. Maurice R. Neville, courtesy of Fort Delaware Society.)

100

Pvt. Horace Knowles of Battery C, 261st Coast Artillery was well known among soldiers for his legendary pranks. One night, Knowles discharged his rifle (loaded with a blank) down a dark corridor. Another soldier, "Lunkhead," positioned himself on the ground opposite. Knowles called for the sergeant of the guard and stated that "I challenged and heard nothing, so I fired." They moved down the dark hallway, spotting Lunkhead. The sergeant said "Horace, you've killed him!" then fainted. Private Knowles served at Forts Delaware, DuPont, and Miles during World War II. (Delaware State Parks.)

Lieutenant Macklin stands in front of the Civil War–era officer quarters, still in use as an office. A sign above the door as well as a few lines on the back of the photograph identify the building as the headquarters for Battery C, 261st Coast Artillery. (Photograph by William A. Smith, courtesy of Delaware Military Heritage and Education Foundation.)

An unidentified visitor plays horseshoes on the parade ground in this photograph taken in the 1940s. Note the stored mines visible on the second tier and two more visitors about to investigate the second floor. With the end of World War II came the military abandonment of Fort Delaware. In 1947, President Truman signed a bill officially turning over the island and fort to Delaware, after 134 years of military activity. (Delaware State Parks.)

# Five

# ABANDONMENT AND
# RESCUE
## 1946–PRESENT

After World War II, Fort Delaware was turned over to the State of Delaware. In 1951, the Delaware State Park Commission became responsible for the fort, and a caretaker was assigned to the island. A group of concerned citizens organized the Fort Delaware Society in the early 1950s to raise public awareness. W. Emerson Wilson and Bill Frank, both newspapermen, regularly wrote about the fort to motivate the community to preserve the historical resource. The "ultimate goal of the Society was to . . . make the fort and island a national park and that pending the achievement of that goal the Society would work to preserve the fort from further vandalism." In 1971, the site was placed on the National Register of Historic Places.

Ironically, historic changes over the years have contributed to the fort's deterioration. The 1870s addition of parapet powder magazines altered the drainage pattern, contributing to water problems within rooms. Compounding the issue, 20th-century vandals ripped out sections of iron drainage pipe. Thus water entered the top of the fort, but instead of being deposited in the cisterns, it invaded the walls and caused extensive damage to mortar and plaster. Efforts at brick re-pointing in the 1960s proved to be cosmetic. Within a few years, the water problem negated the improvements.

Repair of the issue included removing massive amounts of soil from the top of the fort, redirecting drainage through new pipes to the moat, and laying down a modern roofing membrane. The soil was replaced, with care taken to redirect the drainage pattern. With the water problem remediated, it was now feasible to replaster the mess halls beneath using hydraulic plaster. Restoration and period furnishing of a mess hall, the administration building, and other rooms such as the ordnance area and an officers' kitchen provided Delaware State Parks' living history programs an opportunity to bring the fort to life for visitors.

Fort Delaware preservation has come a long way since the 1950s era of a dried-up moat, crumbling brick, rooms overtaken by pigeons, boarded-up windows, and extensive water problems. It stands today as a testament to the many people who lived, worked, or were imprisoned there. The many archival records including photographs, blueprints, letters, journals, and military records will tell this unique story of Delaware's role in the Civil War for years to come.

Although the fort was abandoned, it was of great interest to visitors. Pictured here is a 1950s shot of visiting Boy Scouts on the parapet. Note the tanker passing by in the river and the overgrowth that was consuming the island. (Fort Delaware Society.)

This westerly view of the fort shows a moat consumed by plant life. The parapet also was overgrown with weeds; trees were beginning to grow where cannons once stood. (Fort Delaware Society.)

Fort Delaware's west face (front III) is captured in this snapshot taken from the island's eastern shore. The sluiceway is seen in the foreground, with remnants of a dock to the right. Two modern flagpoles can be seen; by this time, the Civil War pole was out of commission. Around 1900, the army sketched plans to construct additional gun batteries in the area photographed above. Those plans, similar to the Fort Mott batteries across the river, were eventually scrapped due to funding and interest. (Delaware State Parks.)

An early 1950s picture shows an unidentified couple enjoying a leisurely visit in their own boat. There was still no organized boat service to the island. (Delaware State Parks.)

A view of the northwestern fort interior shows buildings with demolished windows, some even lacking frames. Makeshift electrical wires run up the officer quarters into the third floor. Note the tramway tracks running across the parade ground. (Delaware Public Archives.)

More Boy Scouts appear in a photograph of what was probably one of the first tours of Fort Delaware led by the Fort Delaware Society. The gentleman with the moustache is a young W. Emerson Wilson, known to most as "Emmy." Wilson was a charter member of the society and used his influence as a newspaper writer to garner interest in preservation of the fort. (Fort Delaware Society.)

The northeastern side of the fort interior shows more dilapidated conditions. Barely seen above the overgrowth are two groups of 1950s visitors. (Delaware Public Archives.)

Charter members of the Fort Delaware Society in the 1950s stand with a wooden plaque etched with their names. Pictured from left to right are Jefferson Poole, unidentified, John Malone, Anthony Higgins, Murray Metten, Emerson Wilson, and Tom Malone. (Fort Delaware Society.)

On July 24, 1954, organized boat trips to the island began. Pictured here is Walter Wisowaty in one of the earliest boats in service, the *Bobby*. According to the *Wilmington News*, "The first boat will leave at 9 a.m. from Delaware City and the final one from the island will be at 4 p.m. The service is being provided by Capt. Walter Wisowaty and Capt. William Press of Delaware City at a charge of 50 cents per person." (Fort Delaware Society.)

A snapshot shows visitors lining up on the Delaware side awaiting a trip to the island while others disembark the boat. Conditions for loading the boats were less than optimal. Visitors can be seen being helped onto the boat. (Fort Delaware Society.)

This 1959 photograph shows another Wisowaty boat, named *Wiso*, approaching the island. (Fort Delaware Society.)

A barge, the *J. Gordon MacDonough* of Wilmington, Delaware, was sunk adjacent to the island dock on the Delaware side in an effort to stabilize the landing site. Remnants of the barge can still be seen today. (Fort Delaware Society.)

A southern view from the fort entrance shows Battery Hentig in the background amongst overgrowth. Visitors can be seen to the right. Fort Delaware preservation efforts began with clearing the parade ground then working their way up to the second and third tiers. This 1959 photograph shows that the exterior of the fort still had not been improved. (Fort Delaware Society.)

An undated photograph shows Benjamin "Bennie" O'Donnell cutting grass with a tractor; grass is still in the moat, and two trees flourish on the top of the fort. By now, the site was officially a state park; however, it was staffed with only a caretaker. (Fort Delaware Society.)

From left to right, Bill Craven, Thom Alexander, and Rick Bennett prepare to buff a wood floor in the officer quarters in this undated photograph. Craven became involved with fort preservation via his involvement with the Wilmington Jaycees in 1957. In the 1970s, he was president of the society, and he continued to serve the organization for some 50-plus years. (Delaware Historical Society.)

This view of the officer quarters illustrates the condition of the walls and plaster. Note the pocket doors, which are still fully functional to this day. (Delaware State Parks.)

A view of a flashlight-toting tourist standing on top of one of the spiral staircases shows the eastern side of the fort with the sally port entrance in the background. The concrete structure to the left on the ground is the power station for Battery Torbert. (Fort Delaware Society.)

Bennie O'Donnell, seated on the tractor, transports members of the Auxiliary of the Sons of Union Veterans in 1961. Since this photograph, transportation to and from the dock has improved considerably, and guests no longer have to sit on boards placed atop sawhorses. (Fort Delaware Society.)

Interest in the Civil War was enhanced with the centennial celebration in 1961. Although no battles ever took place at the fort, and Confederates never overtook the post, this photograph shows rebels vigorously defending their ground. (Fort Delaware Society.)

When the Fort Delaware Society reached out to community groups for assistance, the Polish Council responded. The group adopted one of the Union mess halls in the enlisted men's barracks, displaying Polish American–related Civil War artifacts and memorabilia. They also had an annual Polish Day at the fort from 1961 until the 1990s. (Delaware State Parks.)

In 1977, Julia Pease, granddaughter of Brig. Gen. Albin Schoepf, visited the fort. She donated items from his personal collection, including his sash and epaulets. (Fort Delaware Society.)

Two Fort Delaware Society members, Walter Wright (left) and Martin Cupery, stand outside the torpedo storehouse in 1979 filling the generator with fuel. The storehouse was adapted to house the generator as well as other maintenance items necessary for upkeep of the fort. (Fort Delaware Society.)

Ray Armstrong, who served as park superintendent from 1965 to 1991, is shown on the dock in front of his park vehicle. Fort Delaware and recently formed wetlands serve as a backdrop. (Delaware State Parks.)

Fort Delaware Society members and volunteers are shown hauling in an artillery piece. The society has worked diligently throughout the years to help return the fort to its appearance as a military post, including enhancing it with period pieces. (Fort Delaware Society.)

A 1979 view of the fort shows visitors taking in a living history demonstration. Due to budgetary restraints and the never-ending flight of pigeons, the second- and third-floor windows of the officer quarters were actually plywood painted to look like windows. (Delaware State Parks.)

An older Emerson Wilson poses in 1979 outside the mine control casemate on the north end of the island. (Delaware State Parks.)

The Fort Delaware Society worked to promote the fort, as can be seen in this 1988 photograph of a roadside billboard. (Fort Delaware Society.)

Polish American volunteers pose on Clean-Up Day 1988 outside the museum known as the Capt. Stanislaus Mlotkowski Memorial Room. Several officers of Polish descent resided at Fort Delaware during the Civil War, including Confederate prisoner Capt. Leon Jastremski. He went on to become mayor of Baton Rouge and later the adjutant general of the Louisiana National Guard. (Fort Delaware Society.)

The proximity of the shipping channel took its toll on the eastern coast of the island. With damage to the seawall from storms as well as shipping, the island began to erode away. In one storm alone, 10 feet of island was lost. The erosion revealed 32-pounder casemate cannon carriages that had been buried on the beach years before. The U.S. Army Corps of Engineers constructed a new seawall as well as funded preservation of the carriages. (Fort Delaware Society.)

A 1988 photograph shows one of the carriages exposed to the elements. Once the carriages were pulled from the shoreline, they were stored in large vats of water in order to stall decomposition prior to conservation. (Fort Delaware Society.)

On November 23, 1990, members of Delaware State Parks and an archaeology crew are photographed during the gun carriage project. The gentleman in the center of the photograph looks down on a carriage resting on its side. (Photograph by U.S. Army Corps of Engineers, courtesy of Fort Delaware Society.)

Park superintendent Ray Armstrong is shown assisting with reclamation of the gun carriages on December 10, 1990. (Photograph by U.S. Army Corps of Engineers, courtesy of Fort Delaware Society.)

A Delaware Army National Guard Huey UH-1 helicopter airlifts a gun carriage to Fort DuPont for storage and conservation. Note the 1897 torpedo warehouse (brick building) visible to the right of the northwest bastion. (Fort Delaware Society.)

Frames were constructed around the carriages in preparation for the lift, and a combination of chains and towropes was employed in the move. (Fort Delaware Society.)

The Fort Delaware State Park office is shown here in 1991, replete with a banner celebrating the 40th anniversary of the park. The park office has since been relocated, and this building is currently a gift shop and ticket office. (Fort Delaware Society.)

From left to right, Kay Keenan, Catherine Jackson, and Jocelyn Jamison, members of the Fort Delaware Society, pose outside the park office. Society members have devoted countless hours both preserving the fort and researching its history. Jamison was instrumental in transcribing prisoner records so that descendants visiting the fort could learn about their family history. (Fort Delaware Society.)

Mike Hitchcock (left) and Lee Jennings, seasonal park interpreters, pause during a living history program in 1994. Enhancement of the Fort Delaware living history program during this time increased park visitorship and garnered key support from legislators. Popularity of the living history program helped to initiate the transition from basic preservation to restoration of the structure. (Author's collection.)

The modern seawall, built by the Army Corps of Engineers, only protects the southeastern side of Pea Patch Island. In February 2010, new erosion is causing damage on the southern (above) and northeastern shores. According to the Army Corps of Engineers, "As ships with deeper drafts evolved, periodic modifications of the channel took place over the years, eventually reaching the current 40-foot depth during World War II." In March 2010, dredging boats entered the Delaware River to begin to carve out a deeper 45-foot depth. (Photograph by Brendan Mackie.)

Restoration efforts included leveling the parade ground, correcting drainage problems on the parapet, carpentry and plaster work, re-creation of a portion of the prisoner barracks, and restoration of the officer quarters. (Fort Delaware Society.)

Peter Morrill (College of Charleston) and Curtis Saunders (Bucknell University) completed the restoration of the auxiliary base end station as an independent preservation project. The base end station is located on the western side of the island, near the modern dock. The structure was built around 1922. (Photograph by Peter Morrill.)

This photograph, taken from the rear of Battery Dodd, looks out over Battery Hentig and the fort. Note the vast improvement in the grounds from the forestation of the 1950s. (Delaware State Parks.)

Living history interpreters such as Rev. Fred Seyfert help to bring the fort alive for visitors. Seyfert, a Fort Delaware Society member, portrays Rev. Isaac Handy, a Confederate political prisoner. (Photograph by Brendan Mackie.)

The AmeriCorps volunteer program plays a vital role in preservation and interpretation of the fort as well as other state parks. Two members are shown here disassembling a damaged footbridge over Battery Allen. (Photograph by Peter Morrill.)

Willis Phelps is one of the most popular and talented interpreters at Fort Delaware. Phelps, a retired Delaware Army National Guard sergeant major, portrays Esau Freeman, a blacksmith apprentice at the fort. (Photograph by Brendan Mackie.)

Fort interpreters pose in this recreation of an 1864 Baldwin Coolidge sketch featuring one of the more unique punishments at the fort. From left to right are Matt Mickletz, unidentified, Joe Dewson, Curtis Saunders, Larry Jensen, Bob Denton, and Peter Morrill. (Courtesy of Peter Morrill.)

The 153rd Military Police Company, fresh from Iraq, visits Fort Delaware during their annual training period. The MPs pose with historical interpreter Sgt. Maj. Michael Golbreski (Retired). (Photograph by Mark P. Del Vecchio.)

# BIBLIOGRAPHY

Burbey, Louis H. *Our Worthy Commander: The Life and Times of Benjamin K. Pierce, in Whose Honor Fort Pierce Was Named.* Fort Pierce, FL: Indian River Community College Press, 1976.

Catts, Wade P., Ellis C. Coleman, and Jay F. Custer. *A Cultural Resources Study and Management Plan for Fort Delaware State Park.* Newark, DE: University of Delaware, Center for Archeological Research, 1983.

Craven, William, ed. "Daguerreotype Received," *Fort Delaware Notes*, vol. 32 (1982): 3–4.

*The District: A History of the Philadelphia District, 1866–1971.* Washington, D.C.: U.S. Government Printing Office, 1976.

Duke, Basil W. *The Civil War Reminiscences of General Basil W. Duke, C.S.A.* Garden City, NY: Doubleday, 1911.

Duncan, William H. *261st Coast Artillery Battalion (Harbor Defense).* Wilmington, DE: Delaware Military Heritage and Education Foundation, 2000.

Fetzer, Dale, and Bruce Mowday. *Unlikely Allies: Fort Delaware's Prison Community in the Civil War.* Mechanicsburg, PA: Stackpole Books, 2000.

Fletcher, William J. *A Soldier for One Hundred Days.* Sarah Fletcher Johnson, ed. Madison, WI: 1955.

*Fort Delaware: March 1898–October 1903, Official Correspondence.* Jocelyn P. Jamison, ed. Delaware City, DE: Fort Delaware Society, 1996.

Gaines, William C. "The Coastal and Harbor Defenses of the Delaware, Part III." *The Coast Defense Study Group Journal*, vol. 10, no. 2 (May 1996): 19–72.

Gihon, John L. *Photographic Colorists' Guide.* Philadelphia: Edward L. Wilson, 1878.

Hagerty, Edward J. *Collis' Zouaves: The 114th Pennsylvania Volunteers in the Civil War.* Baton Rouge: Louisiana State University Press, 1955.

Hamilton, Alexander J. *A Fort Delaware Journal: The Diary of a Yankee Private, A.J. Hamilton, 1862–1865.* W. Emerson Wilson, ed. Wilmington, DE: Fort Delaware Society, 1981.

Handy, Isaac. *United States Bonds; Or, Duress by Federal Authorities.* Baltimore: Turnbull Bros, 1874.

Harding, William W. "Fort Delaware." *The Philadelphia Inquirer*, September 17, 1863: 8.

Hein, Kara K., and Rebecca J. Siders. *A Documentary History of the Arsenal New Castle, Delaware.* Newark, DE: University of Delaware Library Institutional Repository, 1998.

Hollander, Michael. "Fort Mott Guns Aid Salvage Drive." *Flashes*, May 1944: 18.

Jamison, Jocelyn P. "Youngest Prisoners at Fort Delaware." *Fort Delaware Notes*, vol. 46 (1996): 23–24.

Nugent, Washington G. *My Darling Wife: The Letters of Washington George Nugent, Surgeon, Army of the Potomac.* Maria Randall Allen, ed. Cheshire, CT: Ye Olde Book Bindery, 1994.

Park, Robert E. "War Diary of Robert Emory Park." *Southern Historical Society Papers*, vol. 26 (1898): 1–31.

*Seacoast Artillery Weapons: Technical Manual 4–210.* Fort Monroe, VA: Army Field Printing Plant, the Coast Artillery School, 1944.

*The War of the Rebellion: A Compilation of the Official Records of the Union and Confederate Armies.* Washington, D.C.: U.S. Government Printing Office, 1880–1901.

Ward, William W. *"For the Sake of My Country": The Diary of Col. W. W. Ward, 9th Tennessee Cavalry, Morgan's Brigade, C.S.A.* R. B. Rosenburg, ed. Saint Petersburg, FL: The Southern Heritage Press, 1992.

Williford, Glen. "American Seacoast Defense Sites of the 1870s, Part II, Delaware River–San Francisco." *The Coast Defense Study Group Journal*, vol. 21, no. 4 (November 2007): 59–110.

Wilson, Edward L., ed. "John Lawrence Gihon" *The Philadelphia Photographer*, vol. 15, no. 179 (1878): 321–323.

Wilson, Emerson, ed. "Sergeant French at Fort Delaware." *Fort Delaware Notes*, vol. 30 (1980): 3–4.

# Discover Thousands of Local History Books Featuring Millions of Vintage Images

Arcadia Publishing, the leading local history publisher in the United States, is committed to making history accessible and meaningful through publishing books that celebrate and preserve the heritage of America's people and places.

Find more books like this at
**www.arcadiapublishing.com**

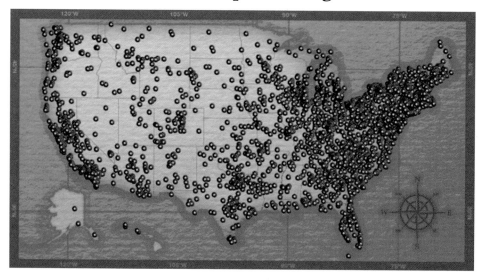

Search for your hometown history, your old stomping grounds, and even your favorite sports team.